Here's what people are s...

Praise for Susie and Otto Collins'
How to Heal Your Broken Heart . . .

"I've had the good fortune to be asked to review *How to Heal Your Broken Heart* by Susie and Otto Collins, and all I can say is Wow. This is easily the best book I've ever read on the topic of getting over a relationship breakup. What sets it apart is its frank honesty and its easy-to-read approach to the subject. Otto and Susie have combined several devices to induce maximum understanding, including a question and answer format, frequent sharing from others who've been through similar experiences, and periodic breakouts of both Otto and Susie's direct perspective on the topic at hand. This combination of approaches gives the reader the impression that he or she is simultaneously attending a seminar, sitting in a support group, and commiserating with a very dear and wise friend. Moreover, the combination of both Susie and Otto's input gives a very balanced male-female perspective on an issue that affects us all, and makes *How to Heal Your Broken Heart* the most universally accessible book of its kind. Kudos! Now I'm sending my copy to a friend in need."

—Dr. Steve Taubman, Author *UnHypnosis: How to Wake Up, Start Over, and Create the Life You're Meant to Live.*

"Every so often I run into people who seem to live out their lives' purpose with passion, conviction and never ending action. I've had the online pleasure of knowing Otto and Susie and their work for the past couple years. They do, indeed, live out and act on their lives' purpose in powerful ways. Here's another example: their newest book, *How to Heal Your Broken Heart: The Secrets to Getting over a Relationship Breakup or Divorce.* Woven with personal stories (yes, you WILL see yourself in some of them) and questions (you most likely are asking) answered from practical personal examples, this is another tool from Otto and Susie that will propel you to another level of relationship growth and health."

—Dr. Robert Huizenga, The Infidelity Coach, www.break-free-from-the-affair.com

"You CAN transform your relationship pain into personal bodacious power! Susie and Otto Collins' practical, honest, and heartfelt advice will show you how."

—Mary Foley, author of *Bodacious! Woman: Outrageously in Charge of Your Life and Lovin' It!*

"A valuable resource of 56 strategies to move beyond the scars of a broken heart."

—Dr. Joyce Buckner, author of *Making Real Love Happen*
http://www.marriage-relationship-advice.com

"Your material has certainly been helpful for me personally and the greatest value was when my ex and I started communicating civilly again. I took the risk and sent him your e-book. It was the first positive response I had from him in 2 years. It felt as though we were both in it together, trying to heal our hearts, rather than adversaries proclaiming more pain than the other."

—Carole Herder

"Yes, this book helped me out tremendously! Although I'm still going through rough times, I have read it I believe three times to keep me out of my funk or as you say staying stuck! I just took a trip and it was pretty dramatic but I brought the part of letting go with me and read the testimonials over and over. I used the breathing techniques to help ease the pain and the thoughts that build up in my head that bring me down. I know I will be in a better place soon. It does take time, however, your book was a big inspiration to me."

—Carol Cooper

How to Heal Your Broken Heart:

The Secrets to Getting Over a Relationship Breakup or Divorce

Susie and Otto Collins

Conscious Heart Publishing
CHILLICOTHE, OHIO

Table of Contents

Acknowledgments

We are very grateful to all of the contributors to this book who so willingly shared their questions and their stories with us and ultimately, with you.

We would like to acknowledge and appreciate all of our teachers, which includes both of our ex-spouses, who have helped us to learn about relationships and personal growth. We are especially grateful for Dr. Belinda Gore who taught us the Power of Presence exercise and much more. We would also like to thank Peri Poloni-Gabriel for the cover design and Janice Phelps for interior design.

Introduction

You may not realize it yet but if you're going through a relationship breakup or divorce now—or you've ever gone through a breakup anytime in your past—your ability to heal your heart, release your pain, anger, guilt and resentment, along with your ability to let go and move on may be the single biggest factor that will determine the quality of love, relationships and for that matter, your overall happiness.

The information we're about to share in this book will not only help you to gain a new understanding for not just the healing process after your break up or divorce, but will help you to make sense of many of the thoughts, feelings and emotions you may be having now or have had in the past.

Sometimes in life, it's helpful to have a guide for uncharted territory or someone to show you the way when the road ahead gets rough.

That's where we come in . . .

Our Story . . .

We've both been through breakups of our previous marriages so we know what you're going through right now. Susie's marriage lasted thirty years and her husband left her; Otto's marriage lasted fifteen years and he left his wife.

Our previous marriages weren't bad relationships, but the life had just gone out of them. Both of us seemed to just drift along for many years, searching for something better and not quite knowing what that something was. We knew it was out there, but didn't have a clue how to create the love we wanted in our own lives.

Both of us have always had a passion for personal and spiritual growth information.

What we began to do, even while we were in our previous marriages, was to read books about people who had the kind of love we wanted and we began to envision what we wanted for ourselves—whether it was with our partners or with another person.

We knew and liked each other through a spiritual group we were part of but were not attracted to each other in any way while we were married to other people. Our marriages ended during the same year, we got together and we had an immediate soul mate experience. Our relationship is the most astounding relationship of love, connection and growth that we ever could have imagined.

Has it always been smooth sailing? Absolutely not. But what we have this time that we didn't have in our previous relationships is a different attitude, different commitments and the tools to create this astounding love every day of our lives.

We each bring different perspectives to the subject of healing after a breakup. We've both had different experiences to reach the point where we found one another and created the wonderful relationship we have now.

It is our intention that the information that we'll share with you in this book will give you the tools, along with the knowledge, courage, strength and feeling of possibility that you too can heal from your relationship breakup, create the love that you want and the best relationships possible.

Ten Steps to Healing . . .

From our experience working with our coaching clients to help them heal and also observing our own healing processes, we have identified ten steps to healing from a relationship breakup or divorce. While we certainly realize that not everyone has to go through these steps and in this order, they are universal enough for us to include this list for you to think about as you work through this book.

With that in mind, here are our ten steps to healing from a relationship breakup or divorce:

1. Realize that it is a choice whether to heal and open your heart again or to stay stuck in your pain and keep your heart closed.

2. Accept your situation for what and how it really is.

3. Allow yourself to grieve on purpose and to feel your feelings. One woman told us that she actually scheduled time each day to cry.

4. Stop the blame game, whether you blame your partner or yourself for what happened in the relationship.

5. Deal with the guilt and begin a forgiveness process, learning to forgive yourself and your partner.

6. Ask yourself in every moment—"What can I learn from this?"

7. Assemble your support group.

8. Begin focusing on your life and your bright future and not on your former partner's life. Ask yourself what you want for your life instead of the pain in the moment.

9. Have faith in God, Spirit or a belief in something greater than you. This faith can help you through the pain of the loss.

10. Start learning from your past and do your relationships differently.

Whether you've just recently been a part of a relationship, or it's been a while since your breakup and you still could use some help in moving forward in your life, we're sure the information we'll share in this book will really be of value to you.

How This Material Is Arranged

As you read through this book, you will see that we have woven these "Ten Steps" within the material. This book is arranged in three sections that correspond to what we perceive the healing process to be for getting over a breakup or divorce. These three sections are "Healing Your Pain," "Letting Go" and "Moving on." They are made up of the top questions from a recent survey we conducted, with over a thousand people responding, plus our answers and advice. In answering these questions, we include our stories, as well as stories from the many people who wanted to share their breakup healing experiences with you. We've also included a fourth section of resources to further help you on your healing journey.

Keep a Journal

As you read this book, you may want to keep a journal and write your thoughts and feelings that come up about healing your broken heart. If you have never kept a journal, it can be especially helpful in processing and getting clear about your feelings and thoughts. It's also good to be able to look back on where you've been emotionally and how far you have come. Your journal can be anything from an attractive, nicely bound volume found at any book store or simply a spiral bound notebook. You can also use your journal to make notes about techniques that you would like to try that are suggested in this book and write your healing goals along the way.

Your Role and Responsibility

It has been our experience that our clients who commit to openness to learning and to putting into action the ideas presented actually succeed in making the changes that they want in their lives.

If this information is to have a lasting impact on your life, we suggest that you make a commitment to being open to doing whatever is necessary to healing from your breakup or divorce.

This may not be easy because it will require risk and effort on your part. If you are willing to stand in your truth, honestly look at your situation as it really is, accept and acknowledge your part in your past relationship challenges, are willing to let go of the past, and live in the present moment, anything is possible.

If you find that you become stuck in your healing process, please know that we offer personal coaching to help with your specific situation.

We are honored to offer you this information that has helped many people and we're sure can help you.

Susie & Otto Collins, Relationship Coaches and Authors

Section 1:
Healing Your Pain

"And yet the grief itself has a way of honing us
and shaping us. It softens us and humbles us.
And then we are more prepared for love."
Marianne Williamson from *Enchanted Love: The
Mystical Power of Intimate Relationships*

If you are reading this book right now, we know that you are probably in a great deal of pain. Although you obviously are aware that many other people have gone through exactly what you are going through, you may think you are very alone when you are in such pain.

When you go through a relationship breakup or divorce, there are usually many different thoughts and emotions happening within you.

You want to know how this could happen to you and why did it have to happen. You want to make sense of your relationship breakup or divorce and you wonder when the pain will stop.

If there is one piece of advice we could give you about healing the pain you have and the questions that keep that pain raw, it's this . . .

Allow yourself to fully and completely feel whatever pain you have, and at the same time, don't allow yourself to stay stuck in your pain.

1

Sound contradictory? *Here's what one woman says about her grieving process after her relationship:*

"I healed my heart by going through the grief process. Yes!! Feel ALL of your emotions as they come because once you allow your emotions to flow through you, they become less powerful. You must feel your pain in order to heal. The grief process can be tricky. Some people develop a relationship with their grief. It is okay to do this, as long as it is a short-term relationship, meaning you do not want Mr./Ms. Grief as your significant other for too long. If so, you do not allow yourself to open your heart to those who enter your life after a breakup.

"Each person deals with grief and pain in their own special way. Cry now, but go out later. Force yourself to do things you do not feel like doing. It increases your will power and strengthens you spiritually and emotionally. I remained focused on myself and figured out what was causing my pain. Usually there are old wounds from childhood that cause us to feel such pain after the loss of a loved one.

"I have developed unconditional love for myself through this process. Yes, SELF-LOVE. It works!! It is God's way. You will be okay!! Go through the pain. Don't try to hide from it. Feel your feelings. And please DO NOT get into another relationship right away. Allow yourself alone time to heal. You will heal. I did not think I would ever feel this good after my last failed relationship. But here I am today, happier than I have ever been in my life. I have control of my life, I have made many new friends and the best part of all is that my heart is WIDE OPEN. I am not afraid to open my heart because I accept myself for who I am. That is the greatest love of all. My prayers are with you. YOU WILL BE OKAY!! Believe and have faith. IT WORKS!!"

In order to heal your pain, we believe that one of the keys is to be as conscious as possible about what you say when you talk to yourself about your breakup.

While we absolutely know that taking your share of responsibility for the breakup and learning from it are very healthy things for you to do, we also absolutely know that continually beating yourself up with negative thoughts toward yourself is not healthy.

For example: Do you love, like and appreciate yourself in spite of what has happened or are you constantly beating yourself up?

Are you continuing to focus on what you lost or are you spending your time focused on what you can learn from this painful situation?

Focusing on "the lessons" that you've learned from a personal growth perspective instead of what went wrong is very important when you are trying to heal the pain from a breakup or divorce.

If you are constantly chastising yourself for failing and putting yourself down without looking deeper at "what did I learn," you will simply draw more experiences to you that reinforce your negative beliefs.

In order to heal your pain, we suggest beginning to pay attention to what you are telling yourself inside your mind. When you catch yourself in a negative, limiting belief (even though there may be some truth to it), change your thoughts to something more hopeful and positive.

We know that this is easier said than done when you are in the midst of a lot of pain, but we urge you to try it. We invite you to get out your journal or a piece of paper and try our self-talk exercise on the next page.

3

Susie and Otto's Self-Talk Activity

Are any of these limiting thoughts and beliefs similar to ones that are spinning around in your head? Write your limiting thoughts and beliefs in your journal.

> "My life is over because of this breakup."
> "I can't live without this person."
> "I'll never have the love I want."
> "There's just one love for everyone and mine just ended so I'll never have another one."
> "I'm unloveable."
> "It's all his/her fault!"
> "It's all my fault because I'm not good enough."

If you could identify with any of those thoughts and beliefs (or any other damaging thought), here are some healthier ones to help you change your thinking:

> "Even though this relationship has ended, I've learned _____ and I'm still okay."
> "Even though I seem to have lost love, there's more or even a better love out there for me."
> "Even though I'm in a lot of pain, I love and accept myself."
> "Even though my relationship has broken up, I have been given a new, fresh opportunity to start my life over."
> "Even though this relationship has ended, I've learned that in a new relationship I want to be different in these ways . . . "

Using our examples, write a more empowering sentence in your journal and start telling yourself this thought whenever the limiting one comes into your mind.

4

Changing your thinking is just a beginning point to healing your pain, but we've found it's a very important step. Whenever you catch yourself thinking negative thoughts toward yourself, your ex, or your relationship that ended, change those thoughts to more positive ones that you can believe. Practice this exercise one moment at a time and watch how you begin to heal.

As you are reading through this section, write down other ideas in your journal that will help you to heal your pain.

With that in mind, here are questions and answers to help you heal your pain . . .

Chapter 1
How Important is Time?

"It's been said that the only thing that can mend a broken heart is time. So the question is— Is time really the most important key to healing after a breakup or divorce??"

In our opinion, one of the biggest myths that exists about how to heal your heart after a relationship breakup or divorce is that time heals all wounds and that it is the biggest factor of all in the healing process.

We all know people who have hung on to anger, grief, and sorrow for many years after a relationship ended and just couldn't seem to move on. It's what you do with that time that determines whether you heal your broken heart or not rather than the time it takes to do it.

Although both of us healed in different ways after our breakups, we each read personal growth and relationship books, went to personal growth workshops, and went to therapy as our relationships ended.

Here's what Susie says . . .

"I went through several months of introspection after my ex-husband left and we decided to get divorced. I wanted to find out who I was, how I had contributed to the breakup, even though he was the one who had found someone else to be with, and discover what I wanted in a new relationship. I also learned about some changes that I needed to make within

myself. Time did help but what helped me more was focusing on my future, what I learned from my past and how I could make positive changes in my life."

Here's what Otto says . . .

"For me, healing has been a process after the end of my previous marriage. Because of the way the relationship with my now ex-wife ended, there was a lot of anger on both our parts. Through it all, the healing process for me has been about learning from the past, reading books, studying spiritual and personal growth materials and learning how to do relationships differently, now and in the future. I've also done a lot of inner work about forgiveness for what my now ex-wife and I did or didn't do to cause our breakup. These are a few of the reasons I teach about relationships because I can help other people learn to do their relationships differently as well."

Sure, time passing can help but you can fall into the trap of thinking that all you need to do to heal is to let time pass. We've found just the opposite to be true. We've found the most important thing you can do to heal is to not shut down emotionally during this time. You want to make sure that you allow yourself to deeply feel whatever you are feeling.

Please understand that we are not suggesting that you intensify the feelings, because that will make the pain worse. What we are recommending is that you simply be present with whatever emotional pain, discomfort, fear or uncertainty that might come up. Allow your feelings to be whatever they are. Allow yourself to go through your grieving process in a conscious way. Get help. Make sure you use the resources we've included at the end of this book. Find a support group or a group of friends to take you by the hand. Work with a coach or therapist. Begin focusing on new possibilities and a compelling future instead of the pain of the past. Honor the good things in your life.

7

Here's what one woman says about her healing process . . .

"Time heals all wounds? For me, it is self-discovery that has healed me—asking the question 'Who are you?' and loving myself. It takes quiet time and that inward knowledge of what brings you satisfaction. This is not an overnight process but it's what you do with the time that is important.

"What did I learn in self-discovery? I learned how I benefited from the breakup. My ex was out-going and I was quiet and shy when I was with him. He was dominant and I shunned all of that. I wanted to be totally behind the scenes while I was married. Since my divorce, I have found my niche and my happiness. Now I'm outgoing, found that I love people and I'm not the same shy person I was when I was in that relationship."

Listen to how another woman helped herself to heal . . .

"What's helped me most was persistently working toward the GOAL of healing for MY sake, forgiving . . . for MY sake. I couldn't let go of anger, hurt, and betrayal. My whining went on endlessly since I had such a whopper to divulge. My counselor gently steered me toward investigating what part I contributed, finding out what I was about (my fears, victimization, negative thinking, projecting, awfulizing, blaming, shouting, etc.) I read every book pertinent to opening up my heart, forgiving, boundaries, undealt childhood issues, etc. I returned to church with an attitude of the desire to become a Christian in lifestyle, not in appearance. I asked for forgiveness from other people I had hurt in the past and acknowledged my deficiencies. Then, most of all, I worked on 'not taking it personally,' realizing that even though his actions seemed they could only be done if I was lowly, unworthy and unattractive, I wasn't. I understand now his bad behavior is a product of his deficiencies and although I was hurt by his lack of love, I am not unlovable. I can love again now that I understand what love is, not what I've made it to be."

Time often can ease the pain, but as you can see, it's what you do with that time that really makes a difference!

Chapter 2
Physical Feelings of Pain

"What about the physical feelings of dealing with a painful breakup? How do I get the knot out of the pit of my stomach? It feels like I have been punched and I can't catch my breath."

There's no question about it—the breakup of a relationship of any kind that's important to you can be very painful. Having a knot in the pit of your stomach and feeling punched is just one way those feelings can manifest. Some people react to trauma with anger, some people withdraw, some people act as if nothing's wrong, some people numb themselves out with alcohol, drugs, television, work, sex, or new relationships—so having this feeling is just one of many ways that trauma can manifest itself and get stuck in the body.

Sometimes life does create circumstances that make us feel like we've been punched in the stomach and can't catch our breath. When something happens that is painful and traumatic, we have to find a way to deal with it that's healthy. It's what we do next after that event that's the important thing.

If you find yourself feeling like you've been punched, can't breathe or practicing unhealthy behaviors, find a way to get in touch with how you are feeling. Since breathing is a totally involuntary response of the body (it does it automatically), if you can't breathe then you are consciously focusing on the fear that is present. If you are eating too much, abusing drugs or alcohol or any other destructive behavior, you are also focusing on fear.

Here's what Susie says . . .

"I remember being in my house and not being able to breathe one day shortly after my ex-husband left me. I was overwhelmed, not only because he left our 30 year marriage and I was alone, but also because now I had the responsibility of the upkeep and repair of our one hundred thirty year old house. My ex had taken care of everything having to do with maintaining or renovating the house, as had my father when I was growing up.

"I had no confidence that I could do the things that they had always done and I felt sorry for myself. I realized that I had always been taken care of when it came to house maintenance jobs and although I was a very self-sufficient person with her own income, it was very hard for me to let go of having a husband around to take care of me in that way.

"Since I couldn't seem to breathe inside the house that day I was overwhelmed, I went outside, lay in my hammock and used every trick I could to calm myself.

"One important thing that I did was to separate the stories that I told myself about my situation from fact. The stories that I told myself came from the fear and low self-confidence that I was feeling at this time in my life. The stories told me that I couldn't take care of my house by myself without my ex-husband here to maintain it. The fact was that many women live in and take care of old houses by themselves. To help get over these fears, I contacted several women friends who were living by themselves in old houses and asked how they did it. Then I took steps to feel more confident by actually doing what they told me. Simply by having phone numbers of repair services and other people who were available for home maintenance helped me to feel secure and to keep breathing."

Separate the facts from your stories and you will untangle the knots and breathe again. By reading this book, you're going to hear how several people calmed themselves and dealt with their fears in order to take steps toward healing. We also invite you to use the techniques that we give you in the resources section of this book. You choose what works best for you. The important thing is to find something that works and taking the first deep breath may be it.

Chapter 3
My Heart Feels Pain

"Why does my heart actually experience physical pain?"

Your heart actually feels physical pain because your feeling center or chakra center in that area of your body is where you feel sadness. When we have great sadness, the area around our hearts can feel very heavy and in some cases like this person, there can be actual physical pain.

If your chest feels heavy and you actually hurt in that area, you probably do want to visit your physician and get it checked out. If your heart checks out okay by your physician, begin taking measures to reduce the amount of stress and sadness that you are holding onto, because if you don't let it go, damage to your physical body can occur.

Begin a yoga or meditation practice. If you are drawn to something more physical, start taking aerobics, Pilates, running, walking—anything to start moving. Get a massage. In the process of moving, you will reduce your stress and the physical pain will probably begin to lessen or disappear in the process. Consciously, start loving yourself and seeing your heart as healthy in your mind's eye. The more you visualize love around your heart area, the less you will focus on the lack of love that you currently feel.

Chapter 4
Why Do I Still Want My Ex?

"Why do you always want to go back, especially after knowing what they did to you? If they are so bad, why do you still want them?"

You want to go back because even though you were in a relationship that caused you a great deal of pain, you want what is comfortable, safe or familiar. It's less frightening to think about the relationship that you had rather than have the hope and confidence that your life would be better without this person. There's something within you that doesn't believe that you can have a better life for yourself. The truth is that in situations like this, it's not so much about what the other person did or didn't do, but your belief in your ability to create what you want. The question to start asking yourself is—what do you want for your life?

Here are two similar questions . . .

"Who am I now that the breakup/divorce has happened?"

"Where do you start? I was widowed, very young."

After a breakup, divorce or the death of a partner, it's normal to feel disoriented in your life because everything has just been turned upside down. The question of who you are now depends on you. You have the choice to be a person stuck in the pain of the past or the person excited about the possibilities of the future. While it's certainly not easy to go from a painful breakup to a thought process of possibilities, this is the work to be done. The fact is—you are a person who can do anything you want with your life if you want to do it badly enough.

The challenge for a lot of people who have gone through a breakup or divorce is that they have tied their identity to a particular relationship or way of being. You are not that relationship. You are someone who was in a relationship and had a set of experiences. Whether you realize it or not, everything you do in your life and everything you experience is as a result of the beliefs you hold and the choices you make as a result of those beliefs.

Who you are now will be determined almost exclusively by what you believe about who you are now that the breakup or divorce has happened. The good news is that if you don't like who you think you are because of the breakup or divorce, you can change it. You or anyone can change the belief you are holding about who you are in light of this one particular event.

The place to begin is to make a list of what you want in your new life and what you want it to look like. Then move toward your new life by allowing it to happen.

Chapter 5
The Pain of Feelings of Failure

"Are there ways to help heal the pain caused by feelings of failure and reduce the self-deprecating thoughts?"

The best way we know to heal feelings of failure and reduce self-deprecating thoughts is to accept the thought that we're all in relationships to learn and to take some time to learn from what happened. Begin by using the self-talk technique that we gave you in the introduction of this section and then take some time and start looking objectively at your relationship that ended.

Ask yourself why this relationship really ended (it may not be what appears on the surface) and then focus on what you learned through this experience.

Take your share of responsibility for the relationship breakup without placing blame on you or your partner.

One of our coaching clients told us about what she learned . . .

"I lived through two divorces and several intimate relationships that ended. My last relationship that ended had been with a very angry man who didn't get along with my family and that was very important to me. After I was able to end this unhealthy relationship, I began feeling like a failure until I made some insightful realizations in one of my coaching sessions with Susie and Otto. I realized that I was briefly in this relationship so that I could learn how to set healthy boundaries with a man, even though he was very angry. In past relationships, I had been afraid of my partner's anger and would always close down and emotionally run away when it erupted. Through this experience, I've learned to say what is true for me, stand up for myself and to get out of relationships when they are not healthy for me. When I realized what I had learned, I was grateful for the experience, even though it had been painful, and I didn't feel like a failure any longer."

So if you are feeling like a failure, we suggest that you discover what you learned from your relationship that ended. Make a list of all the ways that this relationship or marriage has made you better, stronger, and more capable. In other words, look back at this relationship with new eyes to see how it has served you, even though you may still be in a great deal of pain because of it. No matter how small or large, make a list of all the ways that you are better by being in that relationship.

It might be that you realize that you have grown emotionally in some way. It might be that you realize that you need to do some things differently in your next relationship. There's always some learning to be grateful for from all your relationships if you look hard enough. When you find what that learning and growth is, you will not consider that relationship a failure and will quit beating yourself up for what you did or didn't do.

Chapter 6
Stopping Pain Resulting from Anger

"How do you stop the pain of the breakup resulting in anger towards the other person when they are no more responsible for the breakup than I am?"

Please understand that anger can be a natural progression in your healing process. In other words, it's pretty natural for you to be angry when there is a relationship breakup, no matter who is supposedly at fault.

Anger is something that many people don't realize is going on inside of them until the anger starts coming out in other ways or makes them physically ill. In fact, anger is a far healthier emotion than being permanently stuck in resentment or frozen with pain and depression, but you don't want to continue living with that anger.

Here is what Susie says about her anger after her first husband left their relationship . . .

"I actually didn't feel any anger toward my ex-husband, just a lot of sadness about our breakup and fears about my future. I didn't realize that I was angry until several months later, I took a women's self-defense course and had to fight the 'attacker.' It was in that setting that I finally allowed the rage that I had kept down (that hadn't been an acceptable emotion in

my family) to come out as I fought in the class. What a gift it was for me to let my anger and rage out! I think that really helped me to let go of my pain and move on."

Other people know they are angry, but don't know what to do about it.

Here is what Otto says about his anger following the breakup of his first marriage . . .

"As the weeks and months passed, I realized that I was living with a whole lot of anger about the marriage breakup. I was angry because I somehow wanted to be acknowledged that in leaving the relationship, I wasn't a bad person, the pain I caused was justified, and that I wasn't the only one who was responsible for the breakup. In other words, I wanted my ex to acknowledge that in leaving the relationship and causing the breakup of our marriage, I did the right thing.

"As I look back on that period of time when I was holding so much anger about the breakup, I realize that the only one I needed acknowledgement from was myself. I was my own worst enemy because even though I was the one who decided to end my marriage, there was still that 'not so small voice' within me that told me over and over that it wasn't okay for me to break up the family unit for my own happiness.

"It didn't happen overnight but acknowledging my anger and what I was really feeling inside was a big step in my healing process in my relationship with myself and in moving forward to having a great relationship with my young son. I also began to shift my attention from wanting acknowledgment from my ex-wife to loving myself and making my leaving okay. As I shifted my thoughts and attention from wanting approval from my ex to being cordial with her for the good of our son, my anger lessened and our relationship improved."

If you are angrily judging and blaming yourself or your ex, we suggest starting your healing process by first acknowledging that yes, you are angry and that for the time being, that's okay. With that being said, know that anger turned inward or outward for any length of time can and does affect your physical and mental health.

We suggest that you make the intention and commitment to let go of the anger at yourself and your ex. We're talking about acknowledging that you are angry and then allowing those feelings to flow from you. Know that by allowing the anger to move out, it does not mean that you condone what you or the other person did in that situation. It just means that you are willing to move into finding a healing space for yourself and living a happier life.

You can use a breathing exercise of taking deep breaths, meditation, yoga, kick boxing, taking a walk or any number of ways that we include in the resources section of this book to allow your anger to move and not remain stuck. Many times, if it's your intention to move from anger, you can move your body and it will dissipate, just as Susie did in the self-defense class.

Then find ways to start loving yourself and forgiving both of you.

Chapter 7
Anger at Myself for Getting into an Abusive Relationship

"How do I resolve the anger at myself for getting in a relationship with such an abusive man?"

There are many reasons women get into relationships with abusive men. What we know is that continuing to be angry with yourself is only continuing the abuse that this man started. Our advice to you is to begin shifting your focus from how you were in the past to what you want in the future. One way is to begin practicing positive self-talk, like "I was just doing the best I could do at the time and now I know better" instead of calling yourself a fool in your mind. Give yourself permission to begin changing your thoughts about yourself and watch what happens in your life.

Begin working on your self-esteem by taking classes to build your confidence, join groups that will uplift you, and read and watch positive materials. We are assuming that you have left this abusive man and that, in itself, is something to congratulate yourself about.

Start a list of all of your strengths and good points and then remind yourself about them when you start to berate yourself. Only you can change your life and you can begin by learning how to love and accept yourself.

Chapter 8
Replace Pain with Possibility

"How do you replace pain with possibility and positive thoughts?"

The first thing we would tell you is that it's not a good idea to avoid feeling what's going on inside of you about your breakup or divorce. If you are hiding from your pain or just trying to avoid your feelings, then it will be almost impossible to heal your broken heart.

Trying to think positive thoughts alone without acknowledging the pain usually doesn't work. You have to feel and honor your feelings, but not hold on and stay stuck in them.

One of the best ways to do this is by changing what you focus on. In Earl Nightingale's recording *The Strangest Secret*, he said that we become what we think about most of the time. If our focus is on pain and negativity, we get more of that. If our focus is on possibilities for our new life and positive feelings, we'll have more of that.

Here's Susie's story . . .

"My ex-husband and I separated at the beginning of June one year and we spent that entire summer making the decision whether to get divorced or not. It was a very painful time in my life because for one thing, I had never been alone. We decided to get divorced after Labor Day

that year and I felt lost. From the time we separated, all I could think about was him, wondering what he was doing and how he was doing. No amount of positive thinking seemed to help.

"After a few months of this, I remember standing in my living room and from somewhere deep inside me deciding that I was worth more than this obsession with him and his life. What about my own life? I remember physically turning my body away from the pain and looking toward some invisible future. I remember feeling a glimmer of excitement for what I could do with my life.

"I'm not saying that after that I didn't have pain, because I did, but what I also had was a feeling of possibility. That feeling of possibility came from beginning to focus on what I wanted for my future. I stopped clinging to the past as if that past was all my life was about. I began to see that my life could be much, much more."

Chapter 9
How to Deal with "How Are You Feeling?" Questions

"How do you avoid the 'How are you feeling?' questions?"

Although you may be irritated with them, anyone who is feeling concerned enough to ask you that question is probably concerned about your well-being and means no ill intentions. The most important thing you can do when asked this question is to be real, honest and speak straight from your heart without getting into negative stories or an extended monologue, with you playing the victim. No matter how the relationship ended, you have to avoid taking the "victim" role, and one of the ways you do this is by not staying stuck in a story that doesn't serve you. Playing the victim, even though you may feel that you have just cause, only keeps you stuck and won't allow you to move on.

At the heart of this question is the desire to avoid being reminded about what happened and that the relationship ended. We think that avoiding the question isn't the answer, but rather using the question as an opportunity to shift to a more positive place. You may want to say what is true for you in the moment like—"I'm still feeling a lot of pain from the breakup but I'm learning a lot about me right now."

Chapter 10
Why Did I Stay So Long?

"Why did I stay so long?"

It's been said that men leave relationships too soon and women stay too long. We don't know whether it's a global truth or not, but what we do know to be true is that in many situations, one person feels like he/she stayed too long. They stay too long for many reasons—the children, money issues, beliefs about commitments, nothing better to go to, didn't want to give up on the relationship, fear of change, fear of making a mistake, fear of loneliness, embarrassment of failure, fear of letting go of the known for the unknown and not deserving anything better in life.

The question "Why did I stay so long?" is both a dangerous and important question to ask for two reasons:

1) It's important because if you truly want to heal your heart and move forward to your next relationship with more confidence, with as much trust and as much openness as possible, then you do want to know the answer to the question of why you feel you "stayed too long." Since you don't want to make the same mistake again, repeating the same relationship pattern, it's important to ask this question and not just ask the question, but also have the answer to it.

24

This way, if you truly know why you feel you stayed too long, then you have an opportunity to be more conscious in your current and future relationships and not repeat the habitual patterns that caused you to act in ways that resulted in indecision (or at least your perception of it) and act in the future from a more empowered place.

2) It's a dangerous question because you don't ever want to stay stuck in analyzing the past and staying stuck in the whys of what happened. This is one of those questions that can keep you stuck in the pain of the past if you are not careful.

So, exploring this question of why you stayed so long, in our opinion, is useful up to a point. It's probably useful to do some investigating with a therapist if you were in an emotionally or physically abusive relationship too long. There are undoubtedly issues that you need to heal, and in many cases, you may need help doing it.

With that being said, it's important to not get caught up in blaming yourself for what happened in the past, which includes wondering over and over why you stayed too long. Know that staying stuck in it will not serve you as you move forward toward creating the relationships and life you want in the future.

In any case, it's probably a good idea to discover why you stayed, what that relationship was providing for you and then start forgiving and loving yourself, because you were only doing the best you could do at the time. As we have said before, the idea is to learn from the past and not stay buried in it.

Chapter 11
Best Strategies for the Painful Period

"What are the best strategies to get through the painful period?"

This advice may sound counter-intuitive, but in order to get through the painful period you have to become selfish. This means that you have to spend all the available time, effort and energy you can find to nurture and love yourself. Of course, if children are involved in this breakup, you'll need to focus time and energy on them also.

In essence, do anything that will bring you joy. What are the things that you haven't done in a long time that you really enjoy doing? Ballroom dancing? Bowling? Don't go with the idea of meeting a new partner but rather just to enjoy yourself. One man we know started taking dancing lessons after his divorce and is having a great time! Do these things in groups where singles are welcomed. Try something new. Journaling, art, meditation, yoga are all good ways to get through your pain.

It sounds simple, but choose to be with people who bring you joy and don't choose to be with people who bring you down. Try moving toward being with people instead of withdrawing. Most people want to withdraw when they are in pain and that's fine because we all need healing space, but in order to heal, at some point, you'll need to be with people and activities that bring you love, support and joy.

No matter what stage you're at, it's always good to have time for reflection and thought; however, you don't want to spend all of your time there. If you are feeling sorry for yourself, do something—take a walk, take some cleansing breaths and know that this pain is temporary and that you can move through it.

It's been our experience that most people (especially during and after a breakup or divorce) don't do many things that facilitate their own nurturing or don't do things that they love to do. They get so caught up in trying one more thing or one last time to fix the relationship that they don't spend the time, effort or energy to love or nurture themselves.

Now, more than ever, if you want to heal your broken heart, it's critical that you do things to nurture you, bring you joy and that soothe your soul.

Chapter 12
How to Live in a Lonely House

"How do you live in a lonely, quiet, empty house that was full of fun, enjoyment and laughter, not to mention her stuff?"

Your most important job is to learn what helps you to shift from pain and unhappiness to a more positive feeling in the midst of a painful experience. If you are living in the same house where the two of you lived, a big question you'll need to ask yourself is—"Will it serve my healing process more if I move to a new home or apartment or if I stay where I am?"

If you are planning on staying in the house, it might be a good idea to get someone to help you move out a lot of "her stuff" and redecorate. Give it away, sell it—but let it go. Don't hang on to what was. Start with one room—maybe your bedroom—and get someone to help you paint it and change it. Take everything out of the room and only keep what you truly want to keep. One of the first things one of our clients did after her husband left was to get rid of the king-sized bed that they had shared. On the other hand, Susie liked the waterbed that she shared with her husband for almost 30 years, so she kept it but changed the wallpaper in the bedroom.

After clearing one room, go through the rest of the house, from room to room, the same way. It doesn't have to cost a lot of money to do this. Open yourself to possibilities of creating something new.

Although getting rid of "stuff" that reminds you of the relationship is a good start, you also need to focus on your healing in other ways. In our opinion, it's perfectly okay to let go of anything in your life, whether it's a personal belonging or something like a home, as long as it's a part of your healing process. However, we think that getting rid of those things may be just one step in your healing process.

Along with purging the old, you need to start building your new life. Find a new person to laugh with and be friends with. That doesn't necessarily mean a new intimate partner. It just means someone you can meet for coffee, a movie or dinner and who makes you feel good when you are with them. If you have that as your intention and open to the possibility, you will find a friend like this, but you have to begin letting go of what was.

You have to begin spending time thinking about and creating your new life. As painful as it is to think about—you have to start focusing on a compelling future filled with love instead of a potential future filled with the pain that you are feeling in your heart right now.

Chapter 13
Getting over Being with That Person

"How do I readjust to not having that person in my life anymore? I miss the daily interaction, phone calls, spending time together. All of a sudden, I'm alone and feel very lost, and also wonder constantly if the other person is okay and what they are doing."

"How do you get over a long-term fifteen to twenty year relationship in which almost everything you do is about that other person—your whole past—television, radio, hobbies, all of the everyday things that you never realized that were tied to that person?"

When we read these two questions, we are hearing two people who didn't necessarily want the breakup or divorce and are now faced with starting a new life without that person who was the most important person to them.

There's no question about it—this can be a difficult and painful situation and here's the key to moving past these thoughts and feelings into a life that's happy, healthy and full of possibilities.

As we've said before, in order to get over a long-term relationship and readjust to your new life, the real key is to determine what you want that new life to look and feel like to you. You have to begin the process of creating a future that is compelling and a future that is one that you truly want to move toward. If you don't do this, you could stay in a place of mourning and missing that other person forever.

The tough part is making the transition from having someone to share your life with to being alone. You can readjust your life by taking it a moment at a time and opening to finding new ways to be happy and new people to interact with.

If your thoughts are focused on the other person and what he/she is doing instead of you and your life, there's probably a lot of fear and uncertainty within you about your future. In many cases, it's far easier to wonder about your ex than to take charge of your life and begin to live it without that person.

Being with someone for fifteen to twenty years or more and then breaking up is difficult. You might feel like your world has just been turned upside down—and it probably has been.

Here is what Susie says about this . . .

"My ex-husband and I enjoyed sailing for many years before we were divorced. When my husband left, so did the sailboat and an activity that I dearly loved. Sailing made me feel alive. I found that I grieved the end of sailing as much as I grieved the end of our 30-year marriage. Did I have to give up sailing? No, I really didn't. When I came to the realization that I could find a way to go sailing if I chose to, I started to heal that loss inside of me."

When you give yourself permission to do new things, meet new people and even do some things you used to like to do with your ex in a new way, you will be on your way to healing your pain.

Chapter 14

Why Is a Breakup So Ugly?

"How come a breakup has to be so ugly?"

A breakup or divorce doesn't necessarily have to be ugly but unfortunately, in many cases, it ends up being that way and here's why . . .

A breakup doesn't have to be ugly unless both people are invested in the idea that their way is the only way and they are holding onto being right at any cost.

Very often, the real reason for the breakup or divorce actually becomes clearer after you begin exploring your inner feelings after the split. Sometimes these real reasons are much different from the actions that precipitated the breakup in the first place.

The primary reason a breakup becomes ugly is because both people are emotionally tied and invested in the relationship. They still haven't let go. They still emotionally and energetically want from that other person what they didn't get when they were together and what may have caused the breakup or divorce in the first place.

When a breakup or divorce is ugly, it's usually just a continuation and manifestation of what's gone on within the relationship that hasn't been healed. The two people are simply continuing the same dynamics after the breakup that were present when they were together. Acknowledging this fact will help you in your healing process. Identifying your particular "relationship dance" and knowing that it is still going on can help you to stop it.

One of our coaching clients wanted his wife's approval while they were married and continued to want that approval even after their divorce, even though she wanted no contact with him. When he finally realized that he would never have her approval and that he could live without it, he stopped chasing after her and began making a new life for himself.

Realize that if a breakup is ugly, one or both people have chosen for it to be that way. It might be a way of striking back, of penalizing the other person, of holding onto something, revenge, or any number of other reasons.

Know that a relationship breakup doesn't have to be ugly and that it can be a conscious choice for it to be otherwise.

Chapter 15

How Long Will the Pain Last?

"How long will the pain last?"

There's no question about it—if you were in a relationship or marriage for any length of time where there was genuine caring, love and connection, you're probably going to go through pain when you separate.

This pain will last just a short while for some people and much longer for others.

What we've discovered is that the pain will continue as long as you continue doing things that feed your pain. When you stop doing things that feed your pain, then the pain will begin to subside as you begin opening more to your own healing process.

Here are some things that you may be doing that feed your pain and prevent you from beginning your healing process in earnest:

- Resisting feeling into your thoughts, feelings and emotions about the breakup or divorce

- Continuing to hold onto the desire for things to be "the way they used to be" when the clear reality is that this relationship has irrevocably changed form and it won't ever be the way it was.

- Continuing to live in delusion about what really is. For example: "He doesn't really mean this."

- Continuing to foster the desire to strike back or get revenge for what he or she has done.

- Creating stories about what happened to preserve an identity we have for ourselves or a persona we like to project. When we continue to live from an untrue persona, our pain will always continue because we are not living from an authentic place of integrity with ourselves. In other words, we say or act in a certain way to the outside world but we (at some level) know that we're not being who we truly are.

It's been said that we will go to almost any extreme to avoid feeling our true emotions and in many cases, this is absolutely true.

The pain of a breakup or divorce will continue until it is acknowledged, dealt with, understood and healed.

When you can acknowledge the pain, allow it to be there and do things to let it go, your pain will get less and less. You may not realize it but it will.

Read about what helped one man heal his pain . . .

"Get a life, start going places (a new church, weekend retreats, classes, or workshops) and get interested in something. The mind can only think of one thing at a time and the more excitement and fun you have, the less time you'll have to sulk and be a victim. When my interest grows in a sport, hobby, a new friend, there is no pain. I mean no pain. Pain and sorrow grow as we sulk and hold it and talk only about the pain we have. As we develop another interest, we forget and displace the pain with happiness, excitement, or just time filled with something other than pain. We are what we think to some degree. I let that be controlled by my actions. I fill up my days and nights with activity and soon something fun or serious comes up. Meanwhile my pain is diminished by lack of nourishment. Starve the pain and feed the joy."

Chapter 16

Why Do I Let Him Hurt Me Again?

"When someone has hurt you so bad, how do you continue to remember those hurtful moments when they come back around? I find myself falling back on the good memories and forgetting all the hurtful moments, therefore, allowing him to continue to squeeze his way back into my life and hurt me again."

It's our belief that the main reason we come together in relationships, other than love and to enjoy each other's company, is to heal, to learn, and to grow. If you or your partner has decided to end this relationship because the pain outweighs the joy that you experience, then your decision has been made. We're not suggesting that the relationship has to be totally over, but we are saying that if the decision to end the relationship as you knew it has truly been made, then you have to establish some firm boundaries within yourself about what you are and are not willing to accept in your life any longer.

If you allow your previous partner or spouse to squeeze his/her way back into your life and hurt you again, it may be that the lesson you thought you learned already, you haven't learned deeply enough yet.

To illustrate our point, picture yourself waving your hand over the open flame of a burner on a gas stove. Now, the burner can certainly be used for good to cook your food, but it's not good for your hand. You will surely be burned if you continue to wave your hand over the flame and maybe even badly burned.

It might be helpful as you think about this relationship and feel the familiar pull to "give him/her one more chance" to remember our analogy of the burner on the stove.

While it's not harmful to remember the good memories, it is not good if that's all you remember. One very practical and simple way that you can remind yourself of the reality of your relationship is to write down your negative memories in a journal and keep the journal handy so you can read it when you start to idealize your relationship. Along with these not-so-good memories, write about the relationship that you deserve and want to have in your life. Boil it down to one sentence (could be several), something like "I deserve to have a partner who loves me and will listen to me when I talk" and write it on an index card.

Keep that card by the phone, in your pocket, in your purse, refrigerator and desk drawer—wherever you'll be reminded, especially when your ex contacts you. Look at it often and keep your vision for what you want and deserve in your mind and heart. It's up to you to stay in the present moment and look to the future, not getting stuck in what could have been but never was in the past.

Chapter 17

How Do I Get Rid of Good Memories?

"How do I get rid of the beautiful memories we once shared? They are haunting me. How do you get past the things that happen that bring back the good memories?"

If you want to get past the things that bring up good memories, what you're really trying to do is to find a way to shut off the pain. We're not suggesting that you have to forget all of the good memories that happened, even if you could, or to shut off the pain. What we are suggesting is that it is possible for you to step back, look at your good memories as treasures and not reminders of your pain. While we know that it's not always easy to do that until time and healing take place, there are some things you can do to let go.

In order to begin, start doing some things to connect with who you really are. Connect with nature or whatever brings you joy that is not associated with your ex. There's got to be something that you used to enjoy that you didn't share with him or her. It might be a new interest that you would like to explore.

Don't listen to music that brings back memories of your ex. Choose your surroundings carefully and consciously. Consciously choose in every moment what will bring you healing instead of pain.

If you can't or don't want to get rid of reminders like photos, music, and objects that remind you of those beautiful memories, try packing them in a box and putting it away. Start filling your environment with other things. Get help from a friend if you need to.

If you need to stop visiting a certain restaurant, coffee shop or any other place where the two of you created happy memories for awhile, do it. This is probably not something that you have to do forever, but certainly until there isn't any strong emotion associated with the activity or place.

Susie didn't visit one of the lakes she and her ex-husband sailed on for several years because there were too many memories associated with her love of sailing and her ex-husband. Last year, she and her daughter's family went camping on this lake and she didn't feel any strong emotion associated with her ex. Although she still loves sailing, the emotional attachment to her ex and this place was gone.

Even if the pull is great to visit those places again and rekindle your memories, choose different activities for your now that will help you to create other memories.

If you are being haunted by these beautiful memories you once shared with someone, it's going to be very important for you to understand that you can create more beautiful memories in your life, both by yourself and with other people.

In may not be true in every case, but very often when people are haunted by good, positive or beautiful memories, the reason is that they don't believe they'll be able to create more beautiful memories in the future.

Beautiful memories are created when an opening of the heart meets opportunity. Make sure you keep your heart as open as possible to create more beautiful memories in the future. This way, your open heart will invite and accept new opportunities for making memories.

While it's fine to remember beautiful memories, if you want to move forward with your life, it's probably not helpful if you continue to live in those memories. Keep your memories, but start thinking about what you want in your life right now and in your future. There's probably a lot of fear about the future and you might be fearing that you won't have beautiful times in your present and future life. Hanging on to past memories may be a way of you saying to yourself that that's all the happiness I can have and there isn't anymore. The truth is that there is more happiness if you want it.

Start choosing ways to be present with the people in your life and allow a special place for the past, but keep it in the past.

Start creating your vision for what you want in your life and then acting from that place.

Here's how one woman dealt with her memories . . .

"I am 51 years old and have had several hard breakups. However, I had to learn some of my coping skills from my daughter, who was only 20 when she taught them to me. I am in a stable relationship now, so I have learned to love again. After the breakup, my daughter suggested that I make a notebook. Every time I remembered anything at all about 'him' that had hurt, angered, or upset me somehow, I was to write it in the book. In another section of the book I was to write every time I thought of anything I had enjoyed or cherished about him.

"She suggested that instead of looking through old pictures and getting wistful, I should use temporary tape and put up pictures of him that had not turned out well, those where maybe he looked pretty bad in some way. I put the pictures up in places where I would see how 'rough' he looked.

"Every time I would get that look or talk to her in a way that sounded like I was pining, she would say, 'Mom, take that space in your mind and the minute you think about him that way, stop yourself and replace it with ANYTHING. No matter what the thought is that replaces it, just concentrate on that thought until you forget to think about him.' It sounded silly—all this 'teenage' stuff—but it worked.

"I continued to keep writing. It seemed that each time I remembered the good things, I felt that by writing them down, they were kept but after going in the book, they could be discarded in my mind. I eventually realized that I didn't need to keep thinking about them to keep from losing them. They were safe in my memo. My mind could let go of them.

"And when I wrote the bad things down, I no longer had to keep remembering how I was hurting. If I felt like I was craving his memory, I could read from the notes I had written in my HURT section and I would see that I had not lost anything good for me. And if I needed to feel that I had not wasted my time in being in that relationship, I could read from the GOOD memories section and it would remind me that there were reasons that I understood, even though my friends might not have seen why I was in that relationship, that I was not stupid for loving him.

"There were positive things that had happened. I eventually stopped writing in the sections. I was over it. I think it is important to cry and grieve the loss at first. It is a death and if you take a few days to just flat out feel horrible and give credence to that sadness, you will not be stuffing it down. We should never ignore the natural feeling our body tells us to take care of. Crying is curative. And then also if you tell yourself, 'I am such and such years old and I know I am not going to live the rest of my life without an emotion about anyone else. There will be others . . .maybe several more. So I realize that I will love again someday.'

"Put all your keepsakes, your notebook of feelings, and WHAT-EVER else about him you have in a box and store it until you want to throw it away—or not. You know, it is like burying that relationship. I can take out the box now and look at it and I am OK.

"Later I had to learn to trust and not to punish someone else for what a different person had done to me. I didn't give up easily. I got in no hurry. I worked on what there was about me that I didn't like and that took up a lot of time. Now I can love my new man, and I think this time it will last . . . finally!"

Chapter 18

Wasn't I Good Enough?

"Wasn't I good enough? Didn't I do the best I could?"

I f you're one of those people who is going through a relationship breakup or divorce and is asking these questions—"Wasn't I good enough? and "Didn't I do the best I could?"—you should know that these types of questions are what we call endless loop questions. Questions like these will keep you stuck in your pain forever if you continue to ask them.

It's been our experience that everyone always does the best they can do in every relationship, given their knowledge, abilities and level of openness at the time.

Breakups aren't about one person not being good enough or not doing the best he/she could. Breakups and divorces happen because one or both people decide they want different things from the other person in the relationship or that the pain of staying in this relationship outweighs the joy that they are having now and in the foreseeable future. Breakups also happen when one or both people decide they want something different for their lives than what they are currently living.

To the person who is asking these questions—"Wasn't I good enough?" and "Didn't I do the best I could?"—it seems that they are placing most, if not all, of the responsibility for the breakup or divorce squarely on their shoulders alone. They are ignoring or not considering the fact that TWO people make up a relationship and it's two people who can't make the relationship work, not just one.

There is a lot of pain around this question and certainly it's a question that most people ask themselves when they've been left. Even though it is a common question when there's a breakup, we suggest that you not answer it but rather spend time answering two other questions—"What did I learn by being in this relationship?" and "What do I want now for my life experience?" If you don't know what you want for your life experience, start reading some motivational or inspirational books that will help you to find new meaning in your life.

When you refuse to answer the "Wasn't I good enough?" or "Didn't I do the best I could?" questions, you are saying no to being a victim and yes to creating a new life for yourself.

Here is what one woman told us about not feeling good enough and how she healed herself...

"I recently went though a breakup with a man I really loved. I cried for about six months every day. I had to look at my inner child where I was so wounded. It all came down to needing to heal my inner-self. We often get into relationships to heal our relationships with our parents. Due to low self-esteem, I lost my lover. Looking back on it now, the hardest part was putting it into my past because the pain was so raw. I kept telling myself he did not love me and I was not good enough for him. The real truth was I was much more awakened and aware than he was. Even with the experience, I became aware that I had loved with all my heart. I was awake enough to totally love. This part of me inside healed as well and my self-esteem rose. Now when I think of him, I only feel the joy of knowing I can really love, because I really love myself."

Chapter 19

How Do You Get Over Emotional Abuse?

"How do you break up the behavioral patterns that incite people to exploit, misunderstand or abuse you? How does one get over emotional abuse that was within the marriage before the breakup?"

As Eleanor Roosevelt once said, "No one can make you feel inferior without your consent." If you are allowing, or have allowed, other people to exploit, misunderstand or abuse you, then you have the opportunity to put an end to it right now in this very moment. You do this by first saying YES to you and NO to things that others say or do that do not make you feel empowered and uplifted.

If people are exploiting, misunderstanding or abusing you now or in the past, your poor self-worth and poor life choices are allowing or have allowed that to happen. Start to heal by learning to love yourself and by building your self esteem. Know that a person does not get over emotional abuse. A person has to build self-esteem and know that he/she is worth more than to be treated in this way by another person.

What's the best way to build self-esteem?

One way to begin is to write down the behavioral patterns that are keeping you stuck in being a victim and then commit to changing them. Know that patterns, like any habit, can be changed. It just takes persistence and something better to move toward. The "something better to move toward" is the loving you part. When you start loving you and stop doing the things that keep you from loving you, those people who abuse you will not be drawn into your life. You will attract people who will love you like you love yourself.

Start making preferences for your life. Start small, with little preferences like where you'd like to go for dinner, and practice in situations that aren't fearful for you. Take it a step at a time but begin to do it. When you catch yourself saying things like—"Whatever you want . . . "—look within yourself for what YOU want. This advice might sound odd, but when you learn how to state preferences and start creating your life the way you want it to be, you won't attract emotionally abusive people to you because you won't allow them to control you.

One other thing we'll suggest for anyone who has been in abusive relationships in the past is this . . .

Because you've been in an abusive relationship in the past, you will almost have to retrain yourself to open your heart to love again in every single moment when you are attempting to get into a new relationship.

With anyone who has experienced abuse, this is not always easy. So what you have to do is to start repeating a mantra of separation and segmentation with everyone you find yourself in relationship with. This mantra of separation and segmentation is one simple sentence that will change your relationships and change your life if you use it.

The mantra or sentence that you can say to yourself is this: "That was then and this is now."

You say and repeat this sentence to yourself any time you get fearful about opening your heart when the evidence suggests there's nothing to fear. Make sure that you are noticing red flags that tell you that this person is someone to stay away from but don't put up barriers when there's really nothing to fear.

This mantra of "That was then and this is now" will give you the opportunity to bring a new consciousness about choosing partners who don't abuse you, separate the past from your now, and continually give you strength for setting healthy boundaries in any relationship you choose to be in.

Chapter 20

How Do You Forgive and Forget When You Are Hurting?

"How do you deal with trying to forgive and forget when you are hurting so much?"

First of all, when you are hurting so much, it's really difficult to get to a place where you can forgive, let alone forget, about what happened in your past relationship. Forgiveness is a process and having the ability to forgive someone for wrongs that you perceive they have done to you may take some time. For some people, this takes a few days and for others, a few years or never.

As difficult as it is to say and to understand—no one actually wants to cause another person pain. Pain is simply a by-product of someone making a decision about the direction of their life that affects others in painful ways.

What we know for sure about forgiveness is that it isn't about the other person. It's about you. It's about giving yourself the freedom to move from being emotionally closed down, being a victim, being a martyr, or being in pain to having the freedom to choose a happy and fulfilling life.

Before you can forgive, you have to come to an acceptance of the plain reality of what is at this moment in your life. In order to forgive yourself and the other person, you need to get yourself to a place where you understand what you learned by being in this relationship and how being with this person helped make you who you are.

Here's what Susie says about forgiving her ex-spouse . . .

"When my ex chose to stay with 'the other woman' and effectively end our marriage, in order for healing to take place for me, I had to realize what happened in our relationship and take responsibility for my part in it. Even though he left me, I knew that I had played a part in the breakup of our marriage. When I reached that understanding, I began to understand that he was simply trying to find ways to be happier. Even though we had lived congenially together for many years, the passion had died between us and we didn't seem to be connected anymore. He and I both wanted more. I also began to understand that a great relationship with another partner was also now possible and I could find what made me happier. After that realization, there didn't seem to be anything to forgive and I could thank him for having the courage to leave me."

Even though Susie and her ex-husband's breakup didn't create a lot of hatred like many breakups do, we are confident that even where there is a lot of animosity, there can be forgiveness if there is understanding.

You will know that you have forgiven the other person when you have gotten to the place within yourself where there is no emotional charge about your relationship and your ex.

As far as forgetting, we're not sure that you ever forget what happened. Although you may never forget, you will be able to be happy again and move on with your life if you are able to forgive and to understand.

Here's one woman's story about how she used forgiveness to heal a lot of her pain . . .

"For 18 years I was married to a man who physically and mentally abused me. He drank heavily and used to knock me around when drunk. I sort of had the Cinderella complex where I thought you met a man and lived happily ever after. I was always hoping that my love would be able to change him, but of course you cannot change another person. I stayed in this relationship because I was too afraid to leave. Fear of the unknown is very powerful.

"Eventually I got the courage to go when I was at the end of my tether. It was the best thing I ever did, but it left me with lots of pain and no self-worth at all. I needed to build my life up again, so I started to go to assertiveness courses, and self-esteem classes.

"But the main reason I am free from this man now is that I learned how to forgive him. It was not easy, but I just made a conscious effort to do this. He came from an unhappy and sad background himself, and did have some good qualities, so I focused on those qualities. He has now passed away and I went to his funeral knowing that I had forgiven him. I still have some pain, but I am able to deal with it now. I think forgiveness is a major key in recovery."

Chapter 21

How Do You Stop Feeling Jealous of Happy Families?

"How do you stop feeling jealous of other people who appear to be in happy families? I hate going to the park, beach, etc. and hearing all the laughter."

Instead of jealousy, what you really may be feeling is a lot of anger about your breakup. Instead of jealousy, you may be accessing another layer of feelings and emotions you haven't dealt with yet. You may be asking "What about me?" No two people go through the healing process of a relationship breakup the same way and not everyone goes through this.

If you are feeling like you are jealous when you see other people that seem to be happy and have what you had or have what you want, this is a signal from inside you that you need to make a shift.

In order to begin healing, you need to acknowledge your anger—or whatever you are feeling—and go within yourself and deal with it. You may want to re-read our earlier suggestions for dealing with anger.

What your anger or jealousy may be trying to tell you is that you have to change your thinking from failure to possibilities.

Read the story of how one woman changed failure to possibilities . . .

> "I had recently ended a relationship that had many elements that I liked, but the man didn't have the time to spend on our relationship that I wanted. When it ended, instead of feeling like a failure that I once again didn't get what I wanted, I chose to think differently. In the past I would have said to myself, 'What's wrong with me?' But this time, I didn't. I focused on what I wanted the next time around.
>
> "My walking partner was in a great relationship and loved to talk about it while we were walking. Instead of being jealous of her, I loved to hear about her new relationship. As my friend talked, I began getting excited about the possibility that I too could have the relationship that I wanted. As I was walking with my friend, my enthusiasm grew and it wasn't too many months later that I attracted a partner to me who was perfect for me."

So, the decision is up to you. You can decide whether to continue to look at other people who are seemingly happy and be jealous of them or angry—holding the idea that you can never have what they have. A better alternative to that way of thinking is to get excited about what could be in store for you in the future.

Chapter 22

Not Falling Apart
During the Divorce

"How do I not fall apart while going through my divorce so that my ex-husband can not take advantage of me and I get a fair and proper settlement?"

In order to get through a divorce and keep it together when it really matters, give yourself the space and the permission to fall apart.

Here's what we mean by that . . .

Anytime there is a separation and divorce, there is a process of grieving that usually needs to take place, even if it was a terrible relationship. A certain amount of "falling apart" is normal but what you obviously don't want is to do that falling apart when your future depends on it. If this is your situation, one suggestion is to give yourself permission to fall apart, whatever that means to you, once a day or whatever time-frame you need. Sit and devote thirty minutes or an hour to crying, writing and letting yourself grieve about the past. When it counts for you to "be together" and not to fall apart, talk to yourself and tell yourself that you are looking toward your future now and not your past. You might write some affirmations and keep them handy during these times to remind you what you want your future to look like.

One of the worst things you should do is try to go through your divorce or breakup alone. Get the help that you need. If you are concerned that your spouse will take advantage of you because you are not thinking clearly, then you need to assemble a few good support people around you.

Make sure you have a good attorney, a competent therapist, an accountant or tax advisor and as many friends as you can muster to support you in a time when you may not be thinking clearly.

With the proper support and giving yourself permission to grieve, you will find that you have the confidence to not lose it when you really need to keep it together.

Chapter 23

Taking an Honest Look at Yourself

"How do you take an honest look at yourself without condemning yourself?"

In order to feel condemnation for yourself, you first have to feel like you have done something wrong.

Most of us have plenty of voices in our heads and programming from our past that are telling us very loudly that we have made mistakes and what we've done isn't right. You have to ignore that programming from your past and those voices in your head and know that no matter what you did and no matter how painful this situation has become, you did what you thought was the best thing for you at this time in your life.

We suggest that you take an honest look at yourself and your part in the relationship breakup, without condemning yourself, by knowing that there are no mistakes in relationships and in life. Every experience, whether we know it or not, has a meaning for us and we will either get it the first time around or need to repeat it in a different form. Know that we all go through this learning process in one way or another. To condemn yourself is to deny your entire learning process.

Remember when you were young and learning to ride a bike? Susie's grandchildren, ages ten and six, are just now doing that. Remember how shaky you were as you were trying to learn how to get your balance on a "two-wheeler"? Did you get mad at yourself when you couldn't do it? Did other people get mad at you when you couldn't do it the first time around or even the twentieth time you tried it? You might have gotten mad at yourself when you couldn't get your balance, but we'd be willing to bet that you had to drop that self-criticism in order to successfully ride your bike.

We suggest that if you are looking at what happened in your relationship that ended (and you need to do that), you drop all criticism about yourself and look from an outside observer's point of view. If there were things that you could have done better or differently (and in hindsight, there always are), choose to learn from it without blame. When you blame yourself, you keep yourself stuck in the past and you aren't able to make the needed changes in your life. Blaming yourself is the wall you hide behind when you don't want to change.

Learn from the past and move powerfully into your new future!

Chapter 24

Getting Past Pain and Opening to Love Again

"I've always tried to learn something about myself after each relationship that ended but it seems to be getting more difficult. I'm almost to the point where I've pretty much come to the conclusion that I just might prefer to be alone for the rest of my life. How do I get past the feelings of hurt, betrayal, infidelity and cleanse my soul of all that negativity and hurt so I can openly and completely love another human being again?"

If you're reading this, you can probably identify somewhat with this question. Most people who have had a series of relationships that have ended tend to feel this way. Their sentiment is—"What's the use. I'd rather be without a partner if I'm just going to get hurt again." After several times being hurt, it's increasingly difficult to open up yet one more time to love again.

If you can identify with this question, you may have given up on love. This is too bad, because in our opinion, a life without love isn't nearly as beautiful and fulfilling as one with love.

The person who has written this question has made a decision that the things that they believe are possible in relationship are simply not worth all the time, trouble, effort and most importantly, the pain that they believe that will come their way if they try and open to love again.

What this person, or anyone who feels this despair, needs in order to open to someone again is a compelling vision of possibility that is much greater than the potential pain. They need to begin focusing on the good within themselves and a future that is full of possibilities.

As we have said before, when a relationship has ended, we suggest that you take some time and examine what happened and your role in it. That's not to say that you blame yourself but rather try to understand what happened and the patterns that continue to happen in your relationships. Instead of thinking of yourself as a victim, begin to take responsibility for your share of what happened. Even if your partners were unfaithful to you, if you are honest, you can find something to learn about how you might have contributed to what happened.

You might have paid attention to red flags that were shown to you before you became seriously involved with this person. You might have asked for what you wanted sooner in the relationship. You might have been more honest about who you are and what you wanted in a relationship, even though it may not have been what the other person wanted.

If breakups have happened frequently to you, there are patterns of your behavior that you need to look at and heal. It might mean getting some help so that you can move forward. When you start looking at your role in these breakups and making some changes in your life and in your attitude, the hurt and betrayal will disappear. When you stop dwelling on what was done to you in the past and begin learning about what it will take for you to attract the person you want to be with to you, you will begin to heal and move on.

You may not realize that in shutting down the possibility of another intimate relationship, you are also shutting out connections with others. **Hear one woman's story about how she moved past her pain to trust again . . .**

"At one point I had just gotten hurt for the last time I said. I swore I would never fall in love again—that nothing in the world, no one in the world could make me love them because I had so much fear of getting hurt again. I didn't date for a couple years after my last heart break. I had actually convinced myself that I was content to be alone. At least until I realized how alone I was. I was really upset one day when a friend of the family I went to school with since elementary school was picking on me. He realized I was going to cry. When he came towards me, I was expecting him to hurt me and I backed up. He grabbed me in the tightest hug I could imagine and said it was okay and I could cry if I needed to. I tried to push him away and started to cry and he just held me tighter. After I had cried harder than I had cried in a long time, I realized I hadn't only been blocking out having a boyfriend/girlfriend relationship, but I was also blocking out all other types in the process.

"I knew that I needed to stop living in a shell or I would literally die from the pain of being secluded from the people I loved and it would have been all my fault. All I really needed was someone I trusted to show me they cared. I thought of him a lot differently after that day. Now I am happier than I have ever been. A couple months later, after I was slowly getting back into trusting people and letting people back into my life, I asked him if he would be my boyfriend. Of course, even then it was after a long speech of all the reasons he shouldn't date me.

"He said he already loved me after knowing me most of my life and knew who I was—who I was in front of my family, friends, and people I don't know. He knew most of my past, and my life habits. After that, he still loved me. Even if we do not stay together, I know we will still be friends. He helped me realize that

I deserved to be loved and that I deserved to be happy. I also realized that it takes two people to make a relationship work and that I wanted to be loved and to be able to love without fear of pain."

Why do we want to be in relationships anyway?

It's to have more love, more connection and a deeper, richer and more fulfilling life experience than we could have if we didn't choose to get into relationships.

Here what Otto says...

"I have told Susie many times that if I died today, I have had a wonderful life because just to have spent one moment in the bliss of being with her has been worth whatever pain I've had to go through in the past in order to be with her."

Whatever you want in relationships, you can have it and at any age.

While it's perfectly fine to remain single, but whatever you do, don't ever give up on having love in your life because it never gives up on you.

Section 2:
Letting Go

"There are two ways you are empowered by any endeavor: First, when you enter into it with a whole heart; and second, when you let it go with a whole heart."

Alan Cohen from *Happily Even After: Can You Be Friends after Lovers?*

Just as it is with healing the pain, letting go is essential if you are going to move from where you are now to having a happy, healthy and more joyful life.

Letting go is so important because if you don't let go of what was, you can never move forward and create what you want in your life. If you don't let go, creating an outstanding relationship and a happy life will be extremely difficult, if not impossible.

We all hold on to the past and most of the time we aren't even aware of it. We hold on to relationships, old ideas, beliefs and old ways of being and doing things, usually long after these are no longer welcome, wanted or serving us.

We, and almost everyone we know or have coached in our relationship coaching practice, have needed to do some work around the idea of letting go to fully invite the best life possible into our daily experience.

Whether you are still dealing with issues of being the one who left, the one who was left, or even if the relationship breakup or divorce was a mutual decision, there is still a letting go process that needs to happen in almost every person's situation. We're imagining that your situation is no different.

If letting go is so important, then what do you need to let go of?

You need to let go of any thought, feeling, emotion, person, situation, belief, attachment that gets in the way of your being able to be happy and healthy in all aspects of your relationships and life. It means letting go of control over another person or situation because you only have control over your own reactions and thoughts. It may mean letting go of what others expect of you and who you thought you were. It might mean learning to forgive yourself or your ex.

Very often, we secretly wonder what is holding us back from attracting the new love, a new job or career, financial abundance or anything else that we say we want and yet we still have an attachment to the past that won't allow us to move forward.

It's important to note here that when we are talking about letting go, this is not forgetting. Forgetting is like creating selective amnesia about things that have happened or people you'd like to wash from your memory. Letting go is different because you are acknowledging the lesson or role that people, situations and events have played in your life while embracing the possibility of creating a different life for yourself.

If you acknowledge and appreciate something or someone, even if the situation has been painful for you, letting go is much more likely to happen. When letting go happens, it's possible to move on to create a life free from encumbrances and create what you want. Letting go can be (and usually is) a gradual process, along with some major breakthrough moments sprinkled in as well.

Here's what Susie says about letting go . . .

"After separating from my now ex-husband, I realized that I was having a difficult time letting go of the sailing that we had done together for years. We had sold the boat that we owned together and I found that I was grieving the loss of sailing in my life as much as the loss of my marriage.

"In order to let go of sailing with my now ex, I began to make a different life for myself. For the first time, I really focused on what I wanted in my life (besides sailing and a live-in man to do maintenance.) I began attending more personal and spiritual growth seminars and going to where I could be with like-minded people. I learned several breathing techniques that would help me to forgive the past and focus on my future, instead of all the 'what ifs.'

"Letting go to me meant letting go of what my ex-husband was doing, thinking and feeling and his new life with his new girlfriend. Letting go meant letting go of my fears that my daughter and grandkids would somehow like being with her better than with me. Letting go meant changing my thoughts about sailing from 'I can never sail again without my ex' to 'If I want to sail, I will somehow find a way to do it.'

"Letting go also meant stopping my fearful thoughts and calling people who were recommended to me to help with the house and learning how to do some things myself.

"Letting go was an on-going process as I let go of my old life and way of doing things to my bright future and my 'now.'"

Here's what Otto says about letting go . . .

"When my relationship with my ex-wife ended, it wasn't until I was able to let go of the anger toward her for what I perceived she did or didn't do in our relationship and what I would like to have had happened differently was I able to begin to honor her and appreciate her role in my life. I was able to see much more clearly what went right and what went wrong after I could get past much of the anger and judgment.

"Before that, I also had difficulty in accepting my role in the breakup. I was unable to look at and examine my role and contributions to the relationship breakup until I could let go of much of the anger that I felt towards her.

"When I became clear enough to look at my role in the breakup, I remembered that I had attended twenty-six concerts one year before our breakup, most of those without my now ex-wife. I also saw that I had held onto a feeling of superiority because of my lofty goals and spiritual path.

"Letting go of my righteousness, superiority, anger, and guilt of leaving has been a gradual process, with some big 'ah-ha' realizations along the way. I wouldn't have the relationship that I have with Susie now if I hadn't let go of these thoughts and feelings about my past."

As you can see from our stories, the letting go process is a unique process for everyone.

Here's one woman's advice about letting go . . .

"Learn to embrace the process of letting go. It's a lot about self love and accepting the things that people do or say that you cannot change. You have to realize that it is their 'stuff' and you have a choice about whether to let it go or not. We've all had things happen in our lives that have affected us and our self-esteem. You cannot ignore that it happened, but you need to understand it and seek help if you need it.

"You have to let go of the thought that 'This is the way life should be'—that you need to be married or 'with' someone. You can't get hung up on the way society, your family or your circle of friends thinks it should be.

"In my healing process, I let go of some of my old relationships that were negative. It made me realize the individuals I wanted to be around. I don't have the time for people who are not uplifting to me. I need supportive, not judgmental people around me."

Whatever letting go means to you, it is just healthy. We suggest trusting the process of life and embracing life—the uncomfortable times as well as the joyous times.

Don't forget, you have a choice between letting go and not letting go. To begin your exploration around this topic, we invite you to answer these questions . . .

What do you need to let go of in your life? If you don't let go, how will you feel? How will not letting go affect your life? How will letting go affect your life?

Here are some questions and answers about letting go that will help you in your process . . .

Chapter 25

Did We Try Hard Enough
or Was Our Time Up?

**"Did we try hard enough and do I now simply have
to accept that our time together was up?"**

As you're reflecting on the whys of the break up or divorce and trying to make sense of it, it's important to understand that trying hard enough is a totally different thing than trying different strategies. For most people, a relationship that has just ended feels like trying to put a square peg in a round hole. No matter how hard you tried, it just wouldn't fit. This is just the way relationships are sometimes. Sometimes you just can't MAKE them work no matter how much you try.

Strategy on the other hand is a different matter. Sometimes a different strategy might have made a difference at an earlier time in your relationship, but maybe not now.

If the relationship is truly over, it really doesn't matter whether you tried hard enough or not because in order to focus on your healing, you have to focus on what you can do differently the next time, what you have learned from this experience and what you can take into new relationships because of it. Continuing to live with the question of "did we try hard enough" will do nothing for you except keep you going around in this vicious circle and holding on to the feeling of pain because you wanted an outcome that didn't happen.

In relationships and life, we always do the best we can in every situation, whether we consciously realize it or not. If both people do not see evidence that there is an opening to come back together and make their relationship better, then it is wise to accept that your time together is over and that there is much more happiness ahead for you.

Trying hard is usually the wrong direction to take in thinking about making relationships better. We've discovered that a better way of looking at gauging the success of your relationship is how open your heart is to the other person.

Chapter 26

How to Deal with What Ifs and Should Haves

"How do you deal with all the "what ifs" and "should haves" that pop into your mind? How do you stop yourself from thinking that you could have done more and if you had, would it have gotten better?"

This is a lot like saying to yourself, "If I had only bought shares of Company X's stock back in the year whatever, I'd be rich right now." While this is true—If you had bought shares of a certain company's stock in their early days of business, you'd be a lot wealthier than you are now, it certainly isn't going to serve you in moving forward toward creating more wealth to spend very much time agonizing about what might have been had you bought those shares of stock.

If you want more financial abundance, you know that you have to concern yourself with making decisions that will help you create the abundance you want in the future instead of dwelling on the past. You know that a missed opportunity is just that—a missed opportunity. You can't recreate the exact same set of circumstances that would bring that opportunity back.

So it is with relationships.

After a period of reflection of what happened in the relationship and realizing how you contributed to the breakup, what ifs and should haves are usually worthless, guilt-inducing mantras that need to be eliminated from your thoughts if you are to heal your broken heart and have the love you want in your life.

But if you're saying out loud right now as you read this— "But wait! I do know what I should have said or done differently." To that we would say, if you or the other person has shut the door on this relationship, the moment has passed. It may be that you feel you need to somehow tell the other person what you could have said or done differently. While this may be appropriate, it may not change the outcome of your situation. It's time to focus on what you can do to start creating a compelling future for yourself and creating the love and relationships that YOU really want in your life without clinging to the hopes of the past.

It's important not to stay stuck, but to learn from what happened in the past and generally "what if" and "should have" thoughts keep you in a stuck place.

However, "what if" is a wonderful question if you're in a relationship and you ask this question from a place of possibility instead of pain.

We ask the question "what if" on a regular basis, but we ask it from a different perspective—What if we were making a bigger difference in the world? What if we could write a book about healing broken hearts and getting over a relationship breakup? What if we could help people overcome jealousy like we do in our course *No More Jealousy*? What if we could open our hearts more to each other?

If we had continued to ask ourselves "what if" about our previous relationships and continued to stay focused in demise of those relationships with the "should haves," we believe that our mission in life together would not be fulfilled.

What ifs and should haves are never helpful thoughts as you are healing from a relationship breakup. We suggest that you reframe your what ifs and eliminate your should haves in order to let go of the past. It's more beneficial to your happiness and the happiness of those you love to bring yourself into the present and live powerfully from that place.

So, what about the nagging thought that if you had done more, your past relationship might have gotten better?

Wayne Dyer said, "Yesterday is just as over as the Peloponnesian war." In order to let go, you have to start believing that. The biggest question we should all be asking ourselves is what do we want and then be focused on how we can have that instead of placing our intention on the pain and failure of the past. There's no way to go back and change what happened. There's only today and what we do with today depends on what we learned from the past and what we want for our experience right now.

We suggest that you choose to start each day fresh and anew, learning from what you would have done differently. Begin doing those things in your current relationships. If you do, you can begin to live in the now and start creating what you want in your life.

Chapter 27
Dissecting What Went Right or Wrong

"Is there a point when it's no longer beneficial to dissect what went right, wrong, or ask the question 'Should I have stayed'?"

I t's been our experience, both in our relationship coaching practice and in our own lives in previous relationships and marriages, that whenever we or anyone experiences a relationship breakup or divorce, the one thing most of us want to know is the why of the breakup.

Asking yourself this question is always beneficial as long as you're using the asking of this question from a place of growth. In our opinion, there does come a point when it's no longer beneficial to rehash all the minutia of the details of a relationship that ended.

The dissecting needs to stop when your questioning and examining is keeping you stuck in the past and focused on the past to the point that there isn't a window for you to see, feel and create your compelling future. At this point, the questioning is no longer serving you and your highest good.

There are several ways that you can know when it's time to move on in your mind from these questions. Among those are: "Is asking these questions serving me in the process of creating the life I want or is it serving me to stay stuck, being a victim and keeping me focused on the relationship that ended?"

Another question to ask yourself is—"When I rehash what went right, what went wrong and to question whether I should have stayed or not, does it bring up anger about my ex?" If your answer is yes that usually means that you have your own inner work to do and it's not about the other person. If anger is coming up for you, it's difficult to take an objective view. Some of that anger has to dissipate for you to learn from what you have dissected.

If anger is an issue for you, we give you some ways to deal with it in various sections of this book. Check out the resources section for a specific breathing technique that will help you cope with any intense emotion.

What we've found to be most useful when a relationship has ended is to spend some time examining what you could have done differently and then make those changes now in your life. Be that person now that you wish you had been then. Remember that you cannot control how another person thinks or acts. You can't change the past. You can only change you.

Chapter 28

How Does One Give Up
All the Issues?

"How does one give up all the issues? I am happily beyond both my eighteen year long marriage breakups and my eight year long term relationship. I am very happily married, yet I still want to know I was finally understood. Why should I care?"

The only reason someone would still care is if they are still energetically attached and emotionally invested in those previous relationships that they claim they are beyond and claim to have let go of already.

If you can relate to this question, then let us be the bearers of some important information for you—you are NOT as happily beyond your previous relationships and marriages as much as you would like to personally think and believe. You are also not over your previous relationships as much as you'd like to have other people in your life think and believe as well.

If you are still energetically or emotionally attached and invested in your previous relationship, this does not necessarily mean that you want to get back with those other people and attempt another relationship with them.

What we are saying is that you still have some inner work to be done about your connections to those other people you were in relationships with. Until you heal those final layers within you that are still raw, you will be unable to totally give yourself to another person and another relationship because there are still parts of you that are hanging on to those other people.

Even if you've done a lot of personal inner work around your relationship issues, there is very often another layer to be peeled and another layer of feelings and emotions to be dealt with and healed.

If after all these years, you are still wanting to be understood by those previous partners, one possible reason could be that underneath all of that is the secret desire for validation from them. You are wanting validation that you were right. You want validation that you weren't the bad one and perhaps you weren't the only one at fault.

As we talked about in the last section, the only real validation in life that counts is the validation that comes from within you. If you still have the desire to be validated by a person with whom you no longer are in relationship with, then it is very difficult to give yourself 100% to your current partner and it may be time to give all of that up!

Here's what Otto says about wanting validation...

"Because there wasn't a great deal of time between the time I left my ex-wife and the time that Susie and I got together, I was still emotionally bruised and I could only give her as much as I had to give. I discovered first-hand that letting go is a process and at least for me, didn't happen overnight. My relationship with Susie continued to deepen as I continued to let go of my previous relationship and my desire to be validated because I was the one who left. This process of letting go has freed up energy which has allowed me to bring myself more completely and wholly to my relationship with Susie.

"When you want validation from past relationships, it's like these ghosts are hanging around the periphery of your life. I was committing

everything that I was capable of committing in my relationship with Susie, but as long as I was harboring this desire to be validated by my ex-wife, my capacity for opening my heart and truly giving myself to anyone was limited. My love and relationship with Susie has expanded and grown as I have let go. I believe this happens in all other relationships as well."

Whether we know it or not, we all have strands of energy that bind us to other people in our lives. When we constantly feed those strands (even with the desire for validation), they strengthen. Whether we know it or not, our desire to be understood and validated from past relationships keeps us stuck in the past and not fully present in our current relationships.

So how do you let go of wanting to be understood from past relationships? Begin a forgiveness process, of yourself and the other person, and begin to understand that the other person was doing the best he/she could at the time. Search in your heart for a way to forgive and understand. Find something you can appreciate about the other person. What Otto appreciated about his ex-wife was that she was a good mother to his son.

Every time he felt the need to be understood and validated by her, he concentrated on the thought that she was a good mother and told himself that both he and his ex did the best they knew how during their marriage. As Otto made this transformation in his thinking, his relationship with everyone began to change. We invite you to try the same technique and see the changes that can happen in your life.

As you continue to release even more of your attachments to your past relationships, you'll discover more openness toward the other people in your life. Perhaps more importantly, releasing your attachments allows a greater possibility and potential for love, connection and passion than you have had up until now. When you're able to let go of the past even more, you may feel freer, more open to possibilities, more present, more radiant, more attractive or handsome and certainly at peace more than you've ever been.

Chapter 29

When Will I Stop Asking Why This Happened?

"When will I stop asking myself why did this happen? How do I deal with the feeling that I have been robbed of my future happiness, family and retirement?"

There are two ways that people who've been through a breakup or divorce ask themselves the question –"Why did this happen?" As we've said before, one way is when it is asked with the purpose of self-discovery in mind and the other way of asking this question will only keep you stuck in the pain of the past.

When the question is asked from the place that this question has been asked—of wondering how to deal with the feeling that they have been robbed of their future—then this question is not facilitating their healing. Instead, it is continuing to keep them stuck in the lie that they are telling themselves that because of this breakup or divorce, the possibility of future happiness is over.

To the person who is asking this question in this way, we say this . . .

You will stop asking yourself that question whenever you decide that you no longer want to suffer. When you realize that it is more painful for you to continue to suffer and stay stuck in your pain of the past than it is for you to begin your healing process in earnest—that's when you will stop asking yourself that question.

We know that this is painful to hear at this moment, but the truth is that we all have only one moment at a time to live and that's the present moment. If you have any feeling whatsoever that what has happened in the past has robbed you of your future, then you are not living in the present moment.

By focusing on the pain of the past, you are actually projecting this pain into your future life. By doing this, what you're actually saying to yourself is "My past is like this . . . and my future will also be like this . . . "

As the famous speaker Tony Robbins said "Your past does not equal your future." We would add these words to Tony's quote— "Only if you don't want it too." In other words, in every moment, you have a choice to make. This choice is this: what do you want your life to be like?

If you want your future life to be filled with joy and happiness, figure out what would bring you joy and happiness and then consciously move step-by-step toward creating the life you envision for yourself.

Anyone who thinks that their life has been ruined by what has happened in the past is living in that stuck place. Anyone who is living that happy, joyful life is doing so because they have chosen to live there.

You can choose to have regrets about what happened in the past and what you lost, or you can begin changing your thoughts to what you want in your present and future. You can choose to ask yourself this question—"What can I learn from this experience?" and make some changes in yourself or you can hold onto pain. The choice is yours!

Chapter 30

How Do You Fall Out of Love?

"How do you fall out of love? How do you let go of someone who you thought you would be with for the rest of your life, someone who you loved so much, more than anyone else in your romantic life?"

"How do you stop caring for that person? How do you stop yourself from picking up the phone and calling them? How do I stop wondering if he thinks about me still the way I do him? How do you overcome obsessive thinking, let go and get on with life?"

These are all excellent questions and ones that many people live with after a relationship breakup. Whether you are the one who leaves or you are the one who was left, you could still feel love for the other person and care about them. Even if you are in a new relationship, you can have deep feelings for your ex.

So what do you do with those feelings and how do you fall out of love?

We don't suggest falling out of love but rather transforming that love into a different type of love and relationship.

Listen to what Susie says about transforming her love for her ex-husband...

"I had always thought I would be married for life with my now ex-husband. Although the romance had died between us, there was friendship, we lived compatibly together, and we shared a daughter and grandchildren. Even after our separation and divorce, there was a lot of love between us. Although we both knew our divorce was the right thing for us to do, both of us cried when we signed our dissolution papers.

"During the months after our separation, I spent a lot of time wondering how my ex-husband was doing, wanting to call and talk with him and feeling a huge loss of love in my life. I just missed him!

"After a few weeks of feeling sorry for myself that I had been left, I made the conscious decision that I was going to transform the love I had for him from a marriage partnership love to the love for a long-time friend.

"The two of us had chosen to both be part of our daughter's life which meant being together during holiday celebrations and other occasions. To make this work, I had to acknowledge my anger and hurt and allow it to flow through me, without holding onto it. I had to acknowledge and understand that both of us wanted and deserved more from an intimate relationship.

"When I allowed myself to understand that both of us wanted and deserved more, what remained was love and appreciation for what my ex had meant to me in the past and the courage it took for him to leave me. I could be in the same room with him, as well as with his new girlfriend, without mourning the loss of our marriage. I could love him as a friend without feeling attached and I still feel that love today.

"Keep in mind that this was a process that I consciously moved through, largely because of my great desire to have the truly close, connected, loving relationship I now have with Otto."

While we realize that not every situation is as loving as Susie's was, there are lessons for everyone to be learned from her story.

Otto's mother still likes to think of Otto as a six year old because she wants to go back to that reality when she was the happiest. When someone finds themselves living in the past in this way, part of the thinking is that if they let go of the past, the possibility of having a joyful life and happy relationships won't be there. What we have discovered is that the exact opposite is true. It's when you let go of attachment to the idea and ideal of how things used to be that you can move forward to creating a happy life and outstanding relationships in the present and future.

Chapter 31

How Do You Get over the Guilt?

"How do you get over guilt? What can I do so I don't have feelings of guilt that the relationship ended, even if the breakup was a mutual one?"

"What is the fastest and most efficient way to learn to forgive the other person and yourself?"

Guilt and lack of forgiveness are feelings that people carry for years and years and may never let go of. Both emotions affect health, future relationships and the general quality of your life.

In order to get over guilt, it's going to be important to first of all understand what guilt is and how and why we create it in our lives.

Guilt is created when we say or do something that is contrary to the moral code from which we believe that we should be living our lives. In other words, we have certain thoughts, beliefs, attitudes and feelings about what we and others should and shouldn't do and sometimes even we violate our own rules for living. When this happens, the feelings of judgment and restriction and tension that well up within us is what we call guilt.

If you are living in a constant state of guilt, you have to determine whose rules these are that you are feeling guilty about. Are they your rules or are they someone else's or maybe even some religious or social organization's rules?

In order to stop feeling guilty, you have to understand that whether you know it or not, you have changed the rules you're now following in your life and you have to make it okay or give yourself permission to live by those new rules. No one can do it for you. It's your choice—to constantly beat yourself up because you aren't following your old rules or to make it okay to live by your new rules. Once you're able to do this, the guilt will start to lose its power and hold on you.

With that simple understanding of guilt, what you have to do to let go of guilt is to start examining the thoughts and beliefs of those old rules that are in conflict with your own heart and soul, to see where they originated, whose beliefs they truly are, and whether they still serve you or not.

Since feelings come from thoughts, attitudes, and beliefs, if you want to change the way you feel about a certain situation, you have to change your beliefs about it. What is a new, more empowering and accurate belief about this situation? For example, if you hold the belief that "God will hate me because I got a divorce" or "I'll never forgive myself for having an affair," or "I've ruined my children's lives as a result of this breakup," you might consider changing those beliefs.

In order to change a belief that no longer serves you, you have to change what you tell yourself. You have to consciously change your thoughts about the topic. While we recognize that this is not an easy process, we know that it can be done. The trick is to change your self-talk to a thought that you can believe that is more in alignment with the direction you want to go in your life.

Using the examples that we gave you of beliefs that could be holding you back, here are some more positive ones that you may want to try on:

84

Limiting Belief	*More Empowering Belief*
"God will hate me because I got a divorce."	"God always wants the best for me and wants me to be happy, no matter what."
"I'll never forgive myself for having an affair."	"Even though I had an affair that caused a great deal of pain for me and others in my life, I love myself anyway."
"I've ruined my children's lives as a result of this breakup."	"Because of my relationship breakup or divorce, my children will have new experiences that they may not have had otherwise. Yes, they might go through some pain because of my decisions, but they will have new living and learning opportunities that they may not have had otherwise."

For more information about how to change your beliefs, check out the information in the resources section of this book.

Here's what one woman says about the guilt she had about leaving her marriage . . .

"Guilt doesn't automatically go away. It's been a constant process over the past 20 years since my divorce. My ex and I have had no contact for 7 years and just since then have I been able to let all of that guilt about leaving go.

"Since I left, I have done a lot of reading and meditation. I've discovered what my passions are in life and I've built on those. I've spent time in meditation trying to find out who I am. I've learned how to trust in who I am and accept and forgive myself for all the things that could have been better in the past. I've adopted the attitude that that's where my ex-husband and I were in the past and if it happened today, it would have been different."

If you are feeling guilty, ask yourself if you need to ask for forgiveness or to make amends in any way. If you do, then do it. If you can't do it in person, write a letter to the person you hurt or find another way to start forgiving yourself. Take the time you need to learn from this experience and realize what you want to do differently the next time you are in a relationship.

Here's what one person says about her path to forgiveness:

"I divorced after 22 years of marriage. Ultimately what helped me to heal was first being able to express to my partner what I felt. I think it helped both of us come to terms with it and begin to forgive each other as well as ourselves. I went to counseling after the breakup. I read and continue to read anything that helps me understand myself better. It also has helped me to see things clearer without placing blame on myself or someone else. There was a lot more going on under the surface than I realized at the time. I had more pain and fears that I hadn't acknowledged or recognized. So often we focus on forgiving others, and find it so much harder to forgive ourselves. For me expressing myself, getting it out instead of holding it in is important. I keep a journal and there I can write anything. As far as learning to love again; it's not just learning to love again, it's learning to be loved again and trust again. I am learning to open up again to another person, especially someone I love. It has taken time, desire and effort to make changes in myself. I can't change the past, I can't change someone else. I can only change myself. I want love to be richer, fuller, this time around. It is a work in progress."

Here's what another person did to make amends:

"I left a miserable marriage after 9 years and 3 children. Every single moment of the breakup was hate and fighting. After many months, I began to understand that everything within our relationship needed to be healed and the only way to do it was for me to understand my part in this broken relationship and to tell my family about this. So I talked to them all one by one and told them the truth, that I could not go on blaming everything on my former husband and that I wanted to say "I am so sorry for all the hurt I have caused. It was just that I did not know any better. I did the best I could under the circumstances. Can you forgive me? Then I asked all my family how they had felt about the situation they had been in and if they would like to tell me about it. Yes, I got a lot of feedback and some of it hurt, but it helped to clean up the past and bring us closer. Naturally there are setbacks and there are things to work on, but the atmosphere is honest and loving. My former husband and I both understand that we have actually grown as people through this process. In some ways we have made our relationship complete and final without losing respect or depriving our children and grandchildren the right to love and respect their father and grandfather."

If you are very hurt, angry and can't forgive your ex or yourself, you need to start letting those ideas go, because if you hold onto those feelings, they can only hurt you. You have to stand back away from your particular situation for a moment and look at relationships from a broader perspective.

As we said earlier, people come together in relationships to learn lessons, to heal, to become better people, to have joy—any number of reasons. When you realize why you came together with this person and what you learned by being with that person, there is only room for being grateful to the person and for the experience. You may be saying to yourself that you can never be grateful for the experience that hurt you so deeply or one where you hurt someone so deeply. If you learned something of great importance and you are a different person because of it, then be grateful. This realization helps if you need to forgive someone or forgive yourself.

Here's how another person learned to forgive . . .

"How did I manage to heal myself and love again? I have managed to heal myself but I have not really found another great love. I have managed to forgive myself and to forgive the man that has left me for another woman. It was not easy. The mourning period was almost 2 years. I made a list of all the things that I thought were my faults and shortcomings in my marriage which had lasted 25 years. I also made a list of the things that broke my heart and the things that I felt were his fault. I made lists of all the things that I thought were unfair. I took all those lists and I burned them. I made a ritual to forgive and forget and to carry on and to look ahead."

People hang onto guilt and lack of forgiveness for many reasons, but one big one is thinking that their partner should be the way *they* think they should be. We all have ideas of how we want to live our lives and we have to recognize that we cannot force another person to live their life the way we want them to live.

Use your breath to forgive. Listen to what another person says about using a tool that we've used (and we further explain in the resources section) that can help you forgive yourself and others...

"When my ex-husband and I broke up, my friend gave me a book by Pema Chodron entitled, When Things Fall Apart. This book was instrumental in my recovery and healing because it encouraged me to sit with my pain - to really look at it and go through it with courage. The book told me that I was not the only one in the world feeling pain at that time. The book allowed me to feel connected to others feeling a sense of loss. I wasn't alone in my pain. I was going to survive like I had before. It was a dissection of sorts.

"Pema encouraged me not to push off the suffering—experience it now, rather than grieve years down the road. There is an exercise she described called Tonglen. As you breath in, one is to fully experience the pain of the situation, but as you breathe out, release love, happiness, and contentment. It was a purging experience. The Tonglen exercise also helped me to forgive my ex-husband and myself.

"Besides reading supportive books, I had supportive girlfriends, married and divorced, who listened and gave me great advice. I have always been rather competitive with women, but in the long run, my friendships with women helped me heal from my failed marriage. I took ownership of my mistakes. I asked my ex-husband what he believed were my 'issues.' He told me that I didn't accept him for who he was, and that I didn't know what I wanted. It was good information for me to hear so that I could once again start a new relationship."

Turn the page to hear another woman's story of healing . . .

"I healed my heart by accepting that I chose to remain long after I knew I should leave, by examining the areas I could have done better in and acknowledging them, by accepting that sometimes there are no right or wrong choices—just different choices. I had to accept that we were never meant to be together and that it was wrong to continue to make one another miserable by trying to change each other. The most healing revelation was the knowledge that neither of us was meaning to hurt the other and that sometimes one person or situation serves their purpose by moving the other to their next life's purpose or goal. When I married my ex, his self esteem was shot and he was stuck in a dead end job where management did not see his potential. While we were married, I helped him get his life back on track. He also served a purpose in my life. He helped raise my son who was seven when we met. While mistakes were made by both of us as parents and spouses, none were meant to injure the other. Acknowledging this helped me to heal, despite the rocky times we endured as a married couple. When you reach a point where you do more harm than good for each other, it is time to stop trying to change the other person and walk away, without guilt or regret."

If you haven't already started, we strongly urge you to begin your forgiveness process, letting any guilt float away from you while learning from the past. Know that others continue to go through this process to a happy life and you can too.

Chapter 32

Getting to Sleep without Thinking of Your Ex

"How can you get your previous partner or ex-spouse out of your head when you are in bed trying to get to sleep?"

Sleep can certainly be tricky after a relationship breakup. It seems that you might be successful in keeping yourself busy and derailing your thoughts to a certain extent during the day, but when the house is quiet and it's just you in your bed alone, it can become very difficult to relax enough to go to sleep as memories and what ifs take over.

If you are having trouble going to sleep because of your thoughts, you are resisting them. We suggest that you allow your thoughts and fears to be there without resistance. Allow yourself to be present with whatever thoughts and feelings are there, feel them and let them pass through like clouds on a spring day. Although this process may bring up sadness, pain, anger, and questions in your mind, no matter what comes up, just allow yourself to be present with your thoughts without resistance. Check out the breathing technique in our resources section of this book for more details.

Please understand that resistance is a different thing entirely than acceptance and taking on guilt or responsibility that may not have been yours to take on.

If it's clear that these thoughts and voices are pretty strong, get out of bed and take out a journal or notepad and write them down as a way to release or acknowledge them.

Here's what Otto says…

"If I get over-stimulated and have too much going on throughout the day without taking time for myself, what happens is when I lie down to go to sleep, those internal voices are waiting for me to get quiet. They remind me of all the thoughts and things I haven't dealt with throughout the day. What I do is get up out of bed, go find one of my notebooks and write down all the things that are banging around in my head. For me, this could be unresolved conversations I had throughout the day, reminders of things I have to do with certain projects I'm working on, or any of a million other things that I haven't dealt with yet."

The key is to acknowledge the thoughts that you have and do something with them. Don't just let them roll around in your head. A great analogy is to look at your brain as a filing cabinet. When you have thoughts and feelings that keep rolling around in your head, one of your file drawers is open and one of the files is completely over-flowing. Until you deal with your overflowing thoughts and feelings, you will continue to try to stuff more into that drawer and you won't be able to close it. You have to experiment with ways that work for you to get to a more calm and centered place in order for that drawer to close.

Here's what Susie did to help her sleep after the breakup of her marriage:

"*Whenever I couldn't sleep because of thinking about my ex-husband, or worrying about taking care of the house by myself, I would get out of bed and do some breathing techniques and exercises that I learned to help me to be less anxious and to calm my thoughts.*

It also helped me if I exercised during the day and to begin a meditation practice called 'sitting.' I found that as I allowed myself to open to new goals and new ways of looking at my situation, I became more hopeful about my future and I didn't have as much trouble sleeping."

Check out the resources section of this book for an explanation of the "sitting" practice.

Chapter 33

Old Gift Cards from Your Partner

"What do I do with the gift cards that I exchanged with my partner now that we're divorcing?"

Those cards that you exchanged were at one time an expression of feelings of how you both felt in one moment in time. There will probably be a time when you are able to open your heart about this situation enough to appreciate that moment in time without sinking back into it but that may not be true in this moment.

If you truly have the desire to move on with your life, remove them from your sight. We realize that letting go is a process and burning, destroying or giving away things associated with your ex is something that you may not be willing to do in the present moment. If you can't bring yourself to destroy gift cards or anything else that reminds you of your ex, something you might do that has worked for others is to box them up and give them to a trusted friend for safekeeping. We kept a box of old letters for one of our friends for awhile until he was emotionally ready to destroy them himself. You might even box them up, seal the box, put it in your attic with a note to be opened five years from now.

Whatever you do, be kind to yourself concerning things associated with your ex, but also take one step toward letting them go.

Chapter 34

Letting Go of Someone Who's Not Right for You

"How do you let go of someone who you know is not right for you but you keep taking back? How do you completely get rid of a person if you don't want them in your life anymore? How do you avoid being sucked in to giving them another chance? How do I stop all the self-talk in my mind—going over and over things and then forgetting the bad and for some reason only recalling the good which sways you to start to think maybe it wasn't so bad?"

Especially after a relationship breakup, memories are tricky things that we can manipulate to suit our purposes. We can find ourselves either dwelling on the bad moments and forgetting what was good in the relationship or we can find ourselves only remembering what was good and forgetting what wasn't so good. Either way, we can get caught in a trap that keeps us captive in the past.

The problem comes from a belief that what you have in this relationship is all that you deserve and although this person is not right for you, you don't believe that you can have anything better in your life. You hold onto the "devil you know" and what is familiar rather than believe that you can have what you want.

There may be some aspect of this person that continues to intrigue, excite and interest you, in spite of your inner knowing that says that he/she isn't right for you. This could be a part of your "dark side" or rebel that you are tapping into and may be something that was forbidden in the past. If this is the case, you may need the help of a therapist to get at the root of your feelings so you can stop your destructive cycle.

Whatever the reasons that you are hanging on, if you know in your heart that this relationship is not what you want and you want to truly end it, you have to consciously have that as your intention in every moment.

Here's one woman's story about her situation...

"My ex left me saying that he 'needed some time.' After two months he moved on, but I did not know it. He kept calling me and saying that he was almost ready to come back. The whole time he was seeing someone else and then she moved in with him. I guess I was still in love and did not realize that he always came to me and never had me over to his new apartment. Now I know that it was because she lived there. Everyone kept telling me that he was no good and that I was better off without him, but would not tell me the real truth. After over two years of that, I finally blocked his number and have moved on. Cutting off all correspondence with him was the only way for me to get over him. As long as I was talking to him and hearing his voice and his lies, I was still right in that trap. I am now dating a great guy and actually have been to his house, so I know that he is not living with another woman. The only way for me to be able to move on was to finally take control of my situation and end the communication with my ex so my heart could heal and I could move on."

Tom, one of our coaching clients, had been in a relationship with a woman for many years who he considered a friend and someone to do things with. He wasn't in love with her although he thought she loved him in a romantic way. She often came to his house and cooked for him, even taking care of his children on occasion. He didn't want to lose the comfort that he had having her in his life but he longed for a romantic relationship that would be much more.

He tried to break up with her several times, but each time something would happen to get them back together and continue their old pattern. She might bring a pie to his house or he might call her when he needed a baby-sitter or a companion to take to a movie.

He asked us to help him let go of her and the convenience of their relationship so that he could attract a romantic relationship. What we told him was that he needed to discover what needs within himself this woman filled in his life. Once he discovered what those needs were, he could start filling them himself or find other people to fill them.

After telling her "one more time" how he felt, he made sure that he didn't contact her for the things that she used to do for him. He found someone else he could hire as an emergency baby-sitter. He met new people he could socialize with. Every time he had the urge to get back into that comfortable feeling with her again, he reminded himself that this relationship, which was based on each of them getting only part of what they wanted, wasn't fair to either of them. After awhile, he was successful in letting this woman go and he did attract a relationship that was more of what he wanted in his life.

In order to let go of a relationship that is what you don't want, you have to know in your heart what you want and believe that you can have it. When that desire is greater than the desire for the familiar feeling you get with this person who you take back time and time again, you will no longer be tempted to reconnect with them.

If you continually allow someone who you don't want to be with to repeatedly come back into your life, it's really clear that you are settling for second-best because you aren't committed to having what you truly want. You may not be one hundred percent clear about what you want. If you had the clarity about what you wanted and the commitment to stay true, then you would either embrace this person totally and completely, or you would be able to let go of them.

If you are only recalling the good and forgetting what wasn't so good—the reasons you might have left the relationship in the first place—you may want to do some things to remind you of the "bad" and what you want in a relationship. This happens often to domestic violence victims. There's sometimes a tendency to forget the humiliation and physical and emotional pain, replacing it with a rationalization that "he will change" or "it was only the alcohol that was the cause and not the 'real' him." You might even be forgetting the emptiness you feel.

Our suggestion to you is to constantly ask yourself these questions when you are tempted to get back together with this person—"What do I deserve?" and "What do I feel inside that I really want in a relationship?" If you keep these questions in mind, you will be moving into your future and not your past.

We suggest that you make a list of why you left or wanted to leave, as well as what you want in a relationship and how you want to be treated by others. Keep this list handy. Keep it by the phone, your desk drawer or wherever you can see it. You stop the self-talk that pulls you back into destructive relationships by reminding yourself how it really was and what you want differently in every moment. You have to believe that you are loveable and worthy of whatever you want to have as a part of your life experience. This happens one moment at a time.

Chapter 35

How Can It Be Natural to End All Ties?

"After a long period of spending time with someone, getting to know them and building a future, how can it be natural to end all ties?"

What is natural is that people change. No matter how well you think you know someone, you can never completely know them and what they want out of life. So, just because you have spent a long period of time with them and have planned a future, it doesn't mean that this person has the same idea about your relationship that you do.

If one person wants to end all ties with you, it might be too painful to see you and talk with you. Although it may seem incomprehensible to you and certainly not honoring what you had together, it may be much less painful for the person to cut all ties and start a new life.

Although relationships can end and the two people can remain friends like Susie and her ex-husband did, it takes a commitment on the part of both people for this to happen. If one person wishes to end all ties, it takes understanding on the part of the other person in the relationship and not taking it personally. While we don't deny that this is a difficult "pill" to swallow, it's one that is sometimes forced on us.

If your ex wants to end all ties with you, do not blame yourself and hold onto the idea that this is an indictment against you.

Sometimes two people come together in a relationship and it will become clear that they have two separate visions that they want for their lives. It doesn't mean that there isn't love, caring and appreciation for that other person, but sometimes in order to get what one person really wants, they have to let go of something else first.

We've discovered that when a relationship ending is abrupt, it's more about the person who left than it is about the other. Although you may not understand it, you can learn to honor and respect his/her wishes without searching for something that you did wrong to deserve such treatment.

You need to keep in mind that none of us react the same to a relationship ending. We're all very different and have different ways of dealing with a relationship breakup. If this has happened to you, don't take it personally, begin letting go and looking to your future.

Chapter 36

Getting over Your Ex and the Memories

"If I have to get over this person, must he be out of my sight for me to forget him? And if he is out of sight, what if my new boyfriend does something that triggers memories of my ex?"

A s we've said before, we're not sure that we ever forget the important people in our lives and the letting go and "getting over" a relationship is different for each one of us. While it certainly may be easier to "get over" an ex if you don't have to see him or her, we've found that what is even more important is your attitude and how you learn to help yourself.

Here are the words of how one person healed when she constantly ran into her ex...

"After breaking up with my last boyfriend, it took me quite a while to heal especially as he went to many of the same places I did. During this time I became acquainted with meditation and started that. I learned a lot about being able to let go and the meditation helped me heal and made me realize there was a whole world out there. I realized I was over the ex when I walked into a local club one day and he was there and I did not feel anything at all about him. He was just another person there. I felt so free and I was already in a good mood that day, but that made me even happier. I did not go looking for love all over again right away, but gave myself time to do other things and develop new interests. Then about a year later I met my current love and we have been together for over 20 years."

How can you stop getting triggered in a new relationship about previous partners?

What we know for sure is that you will get triggered at some time or another in new relationships with a memory of your ex. Maybe your new partner does or says something that reminds you of your ex.

Believe it or not, this is a way we can heal ourselves. When those memories come up, you have the choice to make whether to lapse into nostalgia, sadness, longing for what could have been, or you can take notice of what challenge this memory is bringing up within you and "be" with the feeling.

This memory is pointing the way to what you need to heal within you. If it's a certain touch or a look that reminds you of your ex, you can take that as a sign that you need to shift more of your attention to your new boyfriend. What do you cherish about this new person?

If a negative memory comes up—let's say your new boyfriend does something that he might not think is a negative thing to do but you consider it negative because of a past relationship, you can talk to your new boyfriend about it, but also you can begin to forgive yourself and your old partner.

When any of us are triggered about past relationships, it's always a sign to not bury those feelings but to take some time with some breathing techniques or other ways to find out what's underneath and let them go.

Chapter 37

The Wedding Vow— Till Death Do Us Part

"How do I get over the vow—'Till death do us part'?"

That's certainly a tricky question, especially for people who take their wedding vows very seriously.

As we were thinking about this question, there seem to be three reasons that might motivate a person to ask it . . .

- Their personal thoughts, feelings and beliefs about that commitment are in conflict with divorce.

- The divorce affects their public identity and persona. The question becomes "What will 'they' think and how will it affect my identity in the eyes of other people?"

- Their religious beliefs say that they are going against God or going to Hell if they get divorced.

When someone is having a conflict within themselves about whether it's right to break their wedding vow and get divorced, there is a conflict somewhere in their belief system. In other words, somewhere within them they have adopted the belief that a divorce is not acceptable.

If this is true for you, some important questions to ask yourself are:

"Whose belief or 'rule' is this?"

"Where did this belief come from?"

And maybe the most important question to ask—

"Is this belief serving me now or not?"

If you are in conflict over this vow, your answers to these questions will give you a good idea about where these beliefs came from and why you might be stuck right now. When you made that vow, you made that commitment because you thought this would be for your highest good. What you did in that moment was to make a choice. What we're suggesting that you do right now is to make a new choice for your highest good and say yes to your own happiness. As long as you hold onto the guilt and pain of breaking that vow, it will be difficult for you to let go and create the life your want.

If you are worrying about what others will think of you now that you are either divorced or getting divorced, we suggest that you shift your attention away from what other people may think and to focus on your own happiness. It is simply impossible to make everyone happy with the choices and decisions you make. Everyone is always coming from their own agenda, thoughts, beliefs and ideals.

As our friend Dottie Asselin always continues to remind us, you are the most important person in your life. No one can climb inside and know what's right for you except for you! Please know that you are important, valuable and you deserve to give yourself the kindness, consideration and compassion that you would give to someone else.

No matter what the reason this vow of "till death do us part" is holding you back, you can ask yourself if you kept all the other vows from your wedding ceremony. Usually there's a phrase of vowing to love and cherish one another. Was that love always present? Probably not, if your marriage ended.

What we're saying is to recognize that many vows were probably broken during your marriage and the "death do us part" vow is only one of them.

We would also ask you to consider whether God or whatever entity you made your vow to would want you to choose a miserable life over promises that could not be kept for whatever reason.

If you are a parent or know anyone who is a parent, would you ever want your child to be miserable, upset and unhappy for an extended period of time? If we are ALL God's children, then the two of us do not believe that God or the Creator wants any of us to be unhappy.

If you still can not get past the religious teachings that suggest that you should never divorce, if you continue to embrace the idea that "till death do us part" means that this relationship is the only one you will have in this lifetime, then please understand that this is a personal choice you are making that will determine your happiness in each moment from now on.

We take a contrarian attitude toward this vow and the two of us did not use it in our ceremony when we got married. We vowed many things to each other and among those vows was the promise to be together as long as we were growing together and until Spirit or God dictated otherwise.

What this vow has done is to make us conscious each day of choosing one another as partners to deepen our love. We hold that as our intention and we do not take our love and each other for granted as we often did in past relationships.

Whether you are holding onto this vow for personal or religious beliefs or maybe even because of how your divorce is being viewed by other people—you have a choice whether to hang onto your pain or to let it go and move onto a new life or not. The choice is yours!

Chapter 38

How Do You Get over a Soul Mate?

"When you have broken up, how do you get over a relationship when you have a strong feeling that that person is your soul mate?"

When someone believes they are with their soul mate and their relationship has broken up, one of the biggest challenges is that they have bought into the mythology of soul mates. The mythology says that there is only one soul mate or perfect partner out there for you.

If you are still hanging on to the idea that the person you are no longer with was your soul mate and you are wondering how this break up could be happening, we can't help but wonder if what's really underneath is a fear that because you believe you were with your one and only soul mate, you blew your chance at love and that kind of love won't come around again for you.

Our views on soul mates are radically different from most people who write or talk about the topic. We've thought and written about soul mates a great deal and what we have determined is that there is more than one soul mate out there for you. In fact, there can be many. We believe that everyone who enters your life is a soul mate whose very purpose in entering your life is to help you to heal, to learn and to grow—to be a better person and to evolve personally and spiritually whatever that means to you.

Our belief, as well as the belief of many others, is that a soul mate can come for a brief time or you can be with that person throughout your lifetime until your death or their death.

Yes, that person may have been your soul mate at one time but if that relationship has broken up or you've gone through a divorce, your time together in that form is probably finished.

Here is Otto's story about a soul mate who came into his life for a brief time:

"After my first marriage broke up, I found myself in a relationship with a woman who I will call a soul mate. From the moment we met, there was a strong connection and an incredible feeling between us. It was almost as if we had been together before and there was something about that feeling that I couldn't understand. Part of the reason for my confusion was that I was having feelings of deep connection with this woman that I just met that I never had in 15 years of marriage with my ex-wife.

"Even though I considered this woman to be a soul mate of mine, the relationship didn't last long. As she and I talked about our relationship a few months after the breakup, we both recognized that her purpose in my life was to be a 'bridge' to the rest of my life. Her role was to give me a vision of what was truly possible in relationship that before then I had never experienced.

"Shortly after that relationship with her ended, Susie and I got together and once again I had the same feelings of a soul mate entering my life. This time, the feeling was even more intense that we were more deeply connected on many levels.

"I appreciate that woman's love and what she did for me and I will be eternally grateful. Without her, my life truly wouldn't be the same, but had I chosen to hang onto a relationship with her, I would not have the incredible relationship with Susie that I now enjoy."

Our advice is to appreciate the gifts this person brought to your life. Recognize how your life was changed because this soul mate was in your life. Also realize that you can attract another soul mate to you who will be more in alignment with what you need to learn or what you need to do at this time.

Chapter 39

How Do I Get Closure
If He Won't Talk to Me?

"How do I get closure if he won't talk to me?"

We can't help but wonder if what's at the bottom of this question is that you have a deep-seated desire to get something from the other person. The only closure we ever truly need is to have the belief that "I deserve to be loved and to be happy and I'm moving toward creating the happiness that I want." Everything beyond that is a desire to perpetuate the stories and patterns that went on when you were in a relationship with that person.

If your closure is dependent on whether he talks with you or not, there is much work to be done about the attachment to that person that you haven't let go of yet.

If there are issues that are unresolved that are keeping you tied to the relationship and your ex-partner will not talk with you, you have to decide how long you want to hang on to those thoughts. You have no control over whether someone will talk with you or not or how that person acts towards you. The only thing you can control is your reaction to the situation.

If you decide that you want to close the relationship by yourself, we suggest doing some work around forgiving yourself and your ex, as well as a symbolic completion.

This symbolic completion can come in the form of writing a letter that you send or not send to your ex. It can be burning something symbolic of the relationship (maybe the letter that you wrote) in a fire pit. As it is burning, bless the relationship and let it go. Be sure to read more about completions in the resources section.

Whatever you decide to do, know that even though you may not have all of the answers to your questions and have unfinished business with your ex, you can move ahead with your life if you begin a forgiveness process and also make one or several completion ceremonies.

Chapter 40

Getting over an Ex when He Visits Our Son Every Day

"How can I get over him if he comes to visit our son virtually every day and unfortunately I have to face him?"

That is an uncomfortable situation and one that requires you to set some healthy boundaries for yourself.

Here are a few questions to ask yourself and ideas for you to consider . . .

1) Does it seem that your ex is really coming to see your son or is he coming to spend time with you? If you feel like he's coming to see you and ignores your son, then it's clear that you can set a strong boundary. That can mean that you can set up the situation so that you do not see him when he comes. It might take some planning, but it can be done.

2) Is there a formal visitation agreement? If not, we'd suggest that you initiate getting one.

3) Depending on how old your son is and the situation, you can arrange that your ex meet your son away from the house. In our area, there is a non-profit organization that offers a supervised place for parents to exchange their children so that they don't have to meet. These organizations are usually used for abusive or potentially abusive situations, but you might look into it, depending on how troubling your situation is.

4) If you are entertaining him while he's with your son, stop doing that. Go to another room and get busy with a hobby or project that you'd like to do.

5) Are you separating out the pain and drama in the past from the pain and drama in the present when he comes to visit? You have to separate what happened in the past with what's going on now. Bring yourself into the present moment and stay there.

6) Are you hanging onto the relationship and enjoying his company even though you say you want to get over the relationship? Sometimes we hang onto what's familiar and comfortable even though it's obvious that it isn't working any longer. Begin looking honestly at your feelings and decide if what you really want is to be back together with him.

We suggest that you open to another way of handling your current situation and if you do, you will feel more empowered and will probably find that you are on your way to getting over that relationship.

Chapter 41

How Do I Get Him to Stop Calling?

"How do I get him to stop calling without being insensitive to his feelings?"

As in the answer to the previous question, if you have a strong desire to limit your interaction with your ex, it's time for you to set healthy boundaries for yourself. Our advice is to be honest with him and let him know that it's time for both of you to move on. Tell him that his calling you is prolonging this healing process for both of you.

You are not doing him any favors by not being honest with him. He may have false hopes of getting back together with you. He may be living in the past and depending on you for more than you want to give at this point. By being "sensitive" to his feelings and making them more important than yours, you may be actually holding both of you back from letting go of the old form of your relationship.

This could very likely be a continuation of your patterns and the "relationship dance" that you did when you were together. You have to become empowered and begin moving toward what you want instead of where you were.

Sometimes you have to set strong boundaries. Here's one woman's story . . .

"Well, I had the benefit of living several hundred miles away, but he kept calling me and had me crying and feeling guilty even though he betrayed me. A great friend watched for months how much of an effect the calls had on me. She pointed out to me, she actually had to yell at me, that I don't deserve the torture. If Matt (my ex) actually loved me as he claimed, he wouldn't be doing that to me. That was an epiphany for me. He knew the pain he was causing and he intentionally made me cry nightly, kept me so emotionally exhausted I couldn't live so I'm bound to him. I told him that if he did love me so much, he'd stop. He was welcome to call me, talk and share, but not manipulate me. And I took control myself of how much I tolerated. When I saw a conversation going that way, I ended it and forced myself to live a little. I won't let a phone call delay my plans to go out with the girls. I planned going out, and I did. And I got all dolled up and danced till I couldn't stand up. I eventually met new guys and even dated a few girls, and finally met the guy I plan on spending the rest of my life with. I filled in Matt of my progress and encouraged him to do the same. The calls became less and less frequent, and I became stronger."

We're not recommending being insensitive to your ex. We are suggesting that you be honest and that can come from a place of love and empowerment.

Chapter 42

Can You Remain Friends
with Your Ex?

Here are a group of questions around the theme of whether you can remain friends with your ex or not...

Is it healthy to stay in touch with or attached to someone after a breakup? How can one make a "clean" break and is it possible to remain "friends"?

How do you separate the love you had for that person as a girl/boy friend or spouse to the new love that you have for them as a friend only and remain sane?

How do you maintain a friendship and at the same time, try to give one another space to heal and let go?

This is an issue that some couples grapple with and other couples don't. Some people find that there is so much antagonism between them that they are eager to never see one another again, let alone be friends.

When there is that possibility of the two people remaining friends, many questions need to be asked and honestly answered.

Here's Susie's experience . . .

"As I think about being friends with my ex-husband, there seem to be several layers to it. When we initially decided to separate, he chose to distance himself from me by treating me like a stranger. At the time, that was very hurtful for me, but looking back on it, distancing himself from me may have been the only way he could cope with leaving.

"After a few weeks of settling into our separation and giving each other plenty of space, we came together at events with our daughter and eventually allowed our relationship to transform into being friends.

"I began calling other people when I needed help and advice about the house and didn't depend on him. That helped create the space that we both needed to begin healing. Although I missed him in other ways, I made plans to be with other people and make new relationships. I also had to realize that his leaving was the best thing for me. I had to begin looking at what I wanted in an intimate relationship.

"When Otto came into my life, he accepted my ex-husband's friendship too and he didn't feel any jealousy associated with our relationship. Otto and I had clear intentions for our relationship and he also understood what my friendship was about with my ex."

We realize that friendship isn't always possible. Here are other peoples' experiences and advice on the topic . . .

"In my personal experience and the experience I've seen of others, the only way to open yourself up to love again after a breakup is to cut yourself off completely from the person who broke your heart. I've experienced, or witnessed too many times the pain someone goes through when trying to remain friends with an ex.,

Remaining in contact with a former flame makes it harder for both parties to move on, makes one less motivated to move on, and gives one a false sense that there is hope for reuniting. As harsh as it sounds, people need a clean break to allow them to heal and be prepared to welcome new and better love into their hearts."

Another person wrote this story . . .

"After being divorced for two years from a thirteen year marriage, I was still very hurt and not willing to get involved in any way again. One day out of the blue my ex-husband called and asked for my forgiveness for hurting me. He had remarried and that one failed too. He realized he had made a bad decision, and was sorry for it. I did forgive him and that freed me. We have become good friends, and enjoy our phone conversations. It is now great for both of us to talk to each other about what goes on in our dating experiences. The secret was forgiveness. We can never truly understand what another person is experiencing or feeling."

Here's what another person told us . . .

"I think that being friends after the breakup has a lot to do with the circumstances of the break up. Although I had been with my husband for twelve years and the breakup was very hard, maybe it was for the best and something we both knew would only help us. We are seven years later very good friends, not only as parents of our children, but on a friendship level as two adults. Sometimes two people are just not made to be together in a marriage or romantic relationship but can have a wonderful nurturing friendship."

Remaining friends with your ex after a relationship breakup, even when both people agree about it, can complicate new relationships, especially if the new partner has a jealousy issue. In our work with people around their jealousy problems, friendships with ex-spouses and ex-partners rank high as major causes of jealousy in new relationships.

When this is the case, the people involved invariably have different ideas of what is appropriate behavior with the ex and the jealous person usually has self-esteem issues to deal with. Clear, honest agreements among everyone involved usually help these situations.

One of our coaching clients hadn't clearly decided that he wanted to let go of his marriage when he and his wife separated, even though he told us that he was. His actions spoke louder than his words. He continued mowing the grass and taking care of household chores, even though he no longer lived in their house. Even though their divorce was almost final, he spent a lot of energy taking care of his wife and then wondered why he was having problems attracting a new partner.

We asked him a couple of questions that may be appropriate in your situation if you are wondering about being friends with your ex . . .

Do you fear going cold turkey from your ex to move on with your life? Do you fear that you don't have enough strength to move on without your ex?

If your answer is yes to these questions, we suggest that you become conscious about what you are doing.

Our bottom line advice about this issue is that it is possible to be friends with your ex, but you need to get really clear about what that friendship means for both of you—how much contact you'd like with one another and the form that that contact takes.

The point is that a friendship with an ex-spouse or ex-lover needs to be clearly defined and you need to be completely honest with yourself about your intentions for this relationship. Too often, people are clinging to the past and have not made completions with old relationships. They fail to re-define those relationships, even when they are in a relationship with someone else.

Decide what you each want your new roles with each other to be and if they are very different, you may not be able to come to a place where a relationship based on friendship is what each of you can comfortably handle. Be very honest about where you are emotionally with your ex and if you are still attached to that person, re-evaluate how you might better let go and move on.

Chapter 43

How Do You Deal with Your Family's Feelings?

"It's hard enough dealing with your own feelings. How do you deal with everyone else's in the family?"

No doubt about it, immediate and extended family members are greatly impacted when relationships break up. While the feelings of those you love are important, how you deal with the breakup and your healing strategy for letting go and moving on is what's most important. You can put everyone else's feelings before yours, but ultimately it's your life and you are the most important person in it. Family members may have their lives changed by your break up, and it's good to help them if you are able, but you need to do what's in your best interest to heal and they need to do what's in their best interests to heal.

The important question here is whose feelings are you responsible for? You're certainly responsible for your own and after that, you don't have a whole lot of control over the thoughts and feelings of other family members. You have to let them have their own experience.

When you are going through a breakup or divorce, it's important to be open and honest about what's going on, especially when it comes to your feelings. Don't hide your feelings, your pain or your grief. Let your family members know that you need or would like their support instead of feeling like you have to support them and help them through your challenges.

Depending on your connection with them and your level of openness to them, you should talk about and reveal as much about what's going on in your life and within you as you are comfortable with. Be sure to let ALL your family members know how they can best support you.

Most people have trouble dealing with situations and feelings that are uncomfortable or painful. Sometimes they are totally present, interested, caring and supportive and other times they can be cold, seemingly uncaring, distant and aloof. Many times when a friend or family member comes off as uninterested or uncaring, it probably isn't because they don't love you or care about you. It may be because they simply don't know the best way to help and support you or how to process their own feelings about the situation.

During an emotional time like a breakup or divorce, even though you may be in a great deal of pain yourself, don't take the little things someone else says personally if it doesn't serve or help you. Just know that they are also trying to make sense of the situation themselves.

You may need to be around people who uplift you, instead of those who only remind you of what's happened in the past. That doesn't mean "divorcing" family members too, as well as your partner. It does mean being discerning about how you spend your time and with whom. Remember, you can't help your family members if you are unable to help yourself. Give yourself permission to do what you need to do—with love.

It's totally different if young children are involved in the breakup or divorce. You have a responsibility to help your young children navigate the murky waters (also known as their feelings) during and after the breakup. To find out more, read the answer to the next question.

Chapter 44

How Do You Explain the Breakup to Your Children?

"How do you explain the breakup to your children and deal with their feelings?"

Since Otto has had to deal with this question, here's what he says . . .

The best advice I could give anyone is that no matter how painful it seems, you have to be completely honest about what's really going on to your children about your relationship or marriage breaking up. This means no sugar-coating or lying to help them live in delusion about the situation. Children, like adults, are amazingly resilient when they have to be. Not only is it more difficult on the children if you're not honest, but also it's difficult for you to begin your healing process if you are not. Being honest doesn't mean telling intimate details about your breakup, but it does mean being as honest as you can be without putting blame on you or your ex.

"The most difficult thing I've ever had to do in my life is to sit there on the couch that day and to explain to my then eight year old son that I was leaving the marriage with his mother and the house where we all lived.

"You also have to reassure them that you love them and that the marriage breakup is not their fault. Be there for them when you say you are going to be there. When at all possible, be as much a part of their lives as you are able to be. Attend their ball games, their school functions and anything else you are invited to participate in. If you aren't invited, ask to be included even if it's uncomfortable to be in the same room as your previous partner. Your presence, attention and interest in their lives will be all they need to know and will prove that you have not lost your love for them."

Young children are no different from anyone else in that they also have a need to understand what's going on and why. Because they are searching for answers for why the breakup happened, they might assign part of the blame and responsibility for the breakup or divorce to themselves when they, in fact, had nothing to with it.

The most important thing you can do to help your children and yourself is to be truthful, open and honest, without laying blame on the other person. Continue to let them know that whatever is happening (or whatever happened), it hasn't affected your love for them. Be sure to talk to them on their level about what's going on and avoid closing your heart and shutting off your feelings about your ex. Not only is it emotionally unhealthy to shut down your feelings and not face them, it could also make a young child feel alone and separate if you are distant, aloof or angry with them, in the guise of protecting them.

This is another big reason why it's so important to feel all your feelings and deal with them as they come up—so you can show your children how to be present with what they are feeling. Encourage them to express what they are feeling, but know that you do not have to take abuse from them, no matter what has happened. Remember, your actions will speak louder than any words, so it's important to follow-through with what you say you are going to do.

Chapter 45

How Do I Feel Okay
without a Partner?

"How do I feel okay and enjoy my life without being in a relationship? How do I not feel insecure without a partner and how do I believe that things happen for a reason?"

That's an excellent question and one that most people, especially those who have been in long-term relationships, ask themselves. The truth is that you don't have to be with a partner to be happy. It is a choice.

Being single again is a major life change and one that requires a whole new set of rules to live by. Many people have to make new friends because many of their old friends are married. Although it certainly is possible to keep those old friends, what we've discovered is that it can become more uncomfortable to fit in with those old groups of people as a single instead of a couple.

Here are some suggestions for moving on as a single person...

- Take some time and discover what you would like to do in your life—what interests you'd like to pursue, maybe there's something you'd like to learn more about. Even though you've probably heard this before, find something that you'd like to get involved in that excites you.

- Don't join groups just to meet a partner. Join a group or take a class for what it has to offer you.

- Choose to be around people who uplift you and make dates with them if you don't like going to events and places without a partner.

- Create new goals for your life. If you have goals, you'll bring new energy and new people into your life.

Feeling okay and not insecure about your new single status may take a little time (and it may not), but if you are actively doing some things to heal and create your new life, it may not take as long as you think.

Here's what one woman says about how to be single after a breakup . . .

"Do a lot of soul searching. Open yourself to spirit. Do everything you want to do but did not do because you were in a relationship. Develop yourself as a single person. You were born single, you can and will survive single. You do not NEED another to fill your emotional cup. Get rid of the need by focusing on your issues and healing them yourself. If this means therapy, DO IT!!

"Many people feel they need another's acceptance to feel good about themselves. It does feel good to be accepted, but you must accept yourself first before the right person can come into your life. Do not look to others to make you feel good about yourself. You are handing them your power.

"I have been through a divorce and since my divorce, I went through another painful breakup. I decided to stay single, figured out why I kept choosing the same kind of partner, and from there, I was able to break that cycle. Now I am happily single, I feel free. I know that I am okay with myself and no longer look to others to entertain me or fill me up emotionally."

We believe that things happen for a reason and usually that reason is for our personal growth, even though we may not be able to see it at the time. If you are having problems accepting the truth of this in your life, take a few moments and list what you learned from this relationship that ended. What gifts did you receive?

So if you received so many gifts from this relationship, why did it have to end? Usually relationships end because one or both people had stopped growing in the relationship and its end was for their highest good.

There are always lessons to be learned when any relationship ends and it's important to take time to decide what those lessons are and how you are going to do it differently in your current or new relationships.

The two of us have realized that we would never have been together and been the people we are now unless we would have been in those relationships that ended. By being in those marriages, we were shown how to make ours better.

That's not to say that you can't get it right the first time around, but we are saying that breakups do happen for a reason, even though it may be difficult to deal with that idea in the moment.

Chapter 46

Dealing with the Fear
of the Unknown

"How do you deal with the fear of the unknown while keeping optimistic and confident about your future?"

Fear of the unknown is pretty natural after a relationship breakup. The way to deal with fear is not to stuff it down and pretend it isn't there, but rather to feel it, allow it to be there, while taking a step forward into your future. That step forward can mean many things and you won't always be optimistic and confident. But as you continue to take steps forward, just like a baby learned to walk, you will become more optimistic and confident about your future.

Fear is certainly a useful emotion. It tells you when there's real danger and when to take another path. But fear can also paralyze you into not letting go and moving into your future. The challenge for you is to be with your fear. If you have honestly looked and there are no bright red flags telling you to stop, than move forward. Letting go and moving forward can be very powerful and it can be very scary.

"One has to come to the realization that nothing in life is guaranteed. Sometimes it is just a matter of accepting that there are risks, feeling the fear and doing it anyway. Having said that, I think one can be more careful when making choices, but most things of value don't always come easily and it just depends on whether one is willing to take risks and again trust one's own judgment."

What seems to happen that keeps us stuck in this place of the unknown and being fearful is that we are focused on the past that is painful, a present that seems scary and a future that we don't know how to bring into reality.

The secret to dealing with the unknown is to start creating a compelling future that you can get excited about and then start doing the kinds of things that will help you create that and bring it forth into your reality.

You deal with your fear of the unknown by changing your focus from what you don't want to more of what you do want.

It's also important to start creating some beliefs about what you want that serve you in creating what you want.

The big question that has to be answered is what do you want?

There are lots of ways you could answer this question and these could include—What do you want your future to look like? What kind of relationships do you want to be in? Where do you want to live—In a house? An apartment? A condo? On the beach? Downtown? In the woods? Etc…

What just happened as you were reading these possibilities for your life? Did you start to expand your thinking about what you want for your future? As you did this, if you were truly focused on the possibilities, we're imagining that your fear of the unknown probably shifted from fear of the unknown to hope or even excitement.

If you found yourself thinking—"There's no way I could live there or have that right now," just know that you may be limiting your thinking about what is possible for you now and in your future.

The great business philosopher Jim Rohn once said that you should let fear be your counselor and not your jailor.

To us, this means to look at things as they are, but the one thing we don't want to ever do is to look at things worse than they ever are.

One other thing that we could recommend that will be helpful in dealing with the fear of the unknown is to find role models for what you think you want for your life experience and do what these people do and start thinking the way these people think.

Read the same books that these people read and attend the same events that these people attend. In order to deal with your fear of the unknown, go to your local library or book store and get books to read about people who overcame great obstacles to achieve great things in their lives.

We're not suggesting that you have to have goals to do things like building a huge business, becoming a philanthropist and giving away lots of money or becoming a well-known spiritual leader.

What we are suggesting is that in order to get over your fear of the unknown, you have to have some purpose that is greater than this moment of fear that will guide you in creating your life.

No matter how bad your situation is, it probably won't compare to the story of W. Mitchell.

W. Mitchell not only survived a motorcycle accident where he was burned over sixty-five percent of his body, but then had an airplane accident, which left him paralyzed from the waist down and left him unable to walk. In spite of these things and many other challenges, he went on to start businesses, create thousands of jobs, become a mayor, run for Congress and is currently a popular speaker and author. He wrote the book, *"It's Not What Happens to You . . . It's What You Do About It,"* as an inspirational tool for helping people see new possibilities for their lives.

Are we suggesting that you need to be like W. Mitchell?—only in the respect that you need to focus on the possibilities for your life and what's good and what's working instead of what's not great yet and what's not working.

In order to let go of your pain, sadness, hurt, betrayal, guilt, your previous partner and the way things used to be—whatever it is that you have a need to let go of—we encourage you to start applying the ideas and techniques that we and others have given you in this section. If you do, you'll be on your way to creating your life the way you want it to be!

To help you on your healing journey, here's a recap of some of the ideas in this section:

- Know that you deserve to have the love that you want

- Understand that it is a process and consciously let go of something that would remind you of your past love every day. Know that little by little, if it's your intention to transform your love for your ex into a different relationship, it will happen.

- Take a class or course in whatever area of your life you think you need it. It might be a jealousy course, a self-defense course, a book on communication or self-esteem. Allow something new to help you through this time.

- Understand that your life and relationship has changed. It's not the same as it was. By continuing to wonder if he/she is wondering about you the way you are wondering about them is not going to serve you as you move forward in your life. Focusing your thoughts and feelings on your ex will only keep you stuck and mired in the past. Letting go has to happen in order for you to start moving toward what you want in your life.

Section 3:

Moving On

" . . . Nobody can break your heart if you love yourself. If your heart was broken in the past, you broke it with the lies you believed about love. Love makes you strong; selfishness makes you weak. Love doesn't hurt. What hurts is the fear, selfishness and control that come from the lies you believe in. If you no longer believe in lies, automatically love starts coming out of you."

Don Miguel Ruiz from *The Voice of Knowledge: A Practical Guide to Inner Peace*

To move on to a happier, more fulfilling life, it's not enough to simply let time pass, but rather to learn from your experience and change your life in empowering ways. Many people think and feel that the whole idea of moving on is akin to turning off a light switch on your past relationship and the pain that has happened between the two of you. If that's the only thing you do, you are ignoring an enormous opportunity to create your life the way you want it to be. If you switch off your feelings, you are hiding from the truth of your life and what really is your experience up until now.

Implicit within the very term of moving on is the idea that you are not going to stay stuck, that you've made a decision to look at your situation that you find yourself in at this moment openly, honestly and courageously and do what it takes to heal that part of yourself to move on to a brighter future.

Moving on can be difficult, painful, hard, unconscious or never happen. It can also be a process of ease, openness and love that unfolds naturally, moment by moment. The choice is up to you.

Moving on doesn't have to mean getting into another relationship or even dating, but it might. It might mean resuming your education. It might be learning more about how to have a great relationship. It might mean making sure your relationship with your child or children stabilizes and improves. It might mean moving to another city. It might mean creating your support system. It might mean forgiving yourself and your ex. It might mean starting a hobby or taking a class that you've always wanted to do—something that makes your heart sing. It might simply mean deciding what you want your new life to look like and then taking one small or maybe a large step forward to having it.

In this section, we are going to share some key ideas and strategies to help you go from where you are in your healing process to where you want to go in creating a new life and new relationships filled with potential and possibility.

Whatever moving forward means in your life, here are our suggestions and the advice from several other people who have healed or are in the process of healing from a relationship breakup or divorce. Take what you want from these suggestions and map out your plan for moving forward.

Chapter 47
Single Biggest Thing to Move On

"What is the single biggest thing you'll need to do in order to move on?"

The single biggest thing is to say yes to you by learning to love, accept and forgive yourself and looking forward to an empowered future instead of staying stuck in a painful past. There are probably many reasons why the breakup happened and you could spend the rest of your life analyzing it if you choose. But if your relationship is truly over, the most important thing you can do is to accept that the relationship is over, learn from the experience, begin focusing on you and how you can create a compelling and promising future for yourself, no matter what has happened in your past.

After a breakup, especially from a relationship that lasted for many years, many people don't know who they are anymore without that other person. Who you are now depends on you. You have the choice to be a person stuck in the pain of the past or the person excited about the possibilities of the future. While it's certainly not easy to go from a painful breakup to a thought process of possibilities, this is the work to be done if you so choose. You are a person who can do anything you want with your life if you want to do it badly enough.

As we have said before, everything you do in your life and every-thing you experience is as a result of the beliefs you hold and the choices you make as a result of those beliefs. Who you are now that the breakup has happened will be determined almost exclusively by what you believe about who you are now that the breakup or divorce has happened. The good news is that if you don't like who you think you are because of the breakup or divorce, you can change it. You, or anyone, can change the belief you are holding about what this one particular event means to you and you can learn to love yourself.

Here are some personal stories to give you an idea of what it means to learn to love yourself . . .

"I learned to love who I am, first and foremost. I was in a very abusive relationship, had three children, and then divorced. Now, six years later, I am trying with a man I loved 'at first sight' which I never believed before I saw him. Over the years I had dated, but if someone tried to get serious, I bolted. I usually went for men who I thought wouldn't dare get serious. I always managed to push them away one way or the other within three months, until I saw for a second time the man I was born to love. We have been together almost a year and getting married soon. I learned to love ME. Not easy. I learned to forgive—truly forgive—not just say it but really feel it. I learned 'we are all human.'"

Here's another person's experience in learning to love herself . . .

"After my husband of ten months decided he no longer wanted to be married, I had to find a way to cope with this loss. I could not do this alone, so I looked to a therapist to assist me through this process called divorce. I needed an outsider to be the holder of hope for me, as I was not in any condition to do this for myself. Hope seemed like a far and distant aspiration considering how hurt and broken I felt.

"I am grateful, though, to my therapist for arming my tool bag and setting me on this path. This was the stepping stone that led to further self-exploration and understanding into my feelings relating to our divorce, as well as others that surfaced along the way. I grieved the loss of my relationship, just as you grieve the death of a loved one. I found myself going through all the stages associated with grief (denial, anger, bargaining, depression, and acceptance).

"At times, I felt like I was working a twelve-step program. Just when I thought I'd overcome a stage, I'd find myself falling back. Being a therapist myself, I found myself assigning homework assignments to keep me focused on the hope. I even wished for the opportunity to sit and talk with my spouse about what went wrong, but we were still too raw to embark on this talk. I would have to find solace in reading, writing poetry, journal, practicing yoga, and surrounding myself with friends and family.

"Finally, it seemed as though the clouds had parted and I had reached a plateau. Within this process of letting go, it required me to take stock of my role in the breakup of our marriage, as well as forgiving myself and my spouse. I just kept reminding myself that forgiving never means forgetting, but it gives us the opportunity to move forward.

"My journey of self-exploration and questioning took me to a place of acceptance. I embarked on reshaping my life into one that would bring me happiness, letting go of the hurt, disappointment, and anger. I've always been a firm believer and continue to be one that it takes much more energy to remain angry or hold a grudge than it does to forgive.

"Now eight months later, I emerge a renewed person. I am ready to embrace love and relationships again. I know that where I stand today could not have been possible had it not been for the support and strength of friends and family. I still hold the dream of finding a partner, the one I can share forever with. While my scars are healing, I tread lightly as I accept this new life and challenge. "Through this storm, I found myself again and take one day at a time. Things in life always seem to come full circle and in my case, they most definitely have. I'd like to share with you a quote I came across recently on a piece of jewelry. It's a quote that sums up my new perspective on life: 'Hope is a desire with the expectation of accomplishment.' I'm accomplishing what I set out to do at the beginning of this journey called divorce – embrace hope."

Saying yes to you may mean building your self-confidence.

Here's a short example of how one person built more self-confidence after a relationship breakup . . .

"I went on an adventure with my children, doing things that we had never done before. This built my confidence and self-esteem and allowed me to become more open and confident to a new relationship."

Here's what another person wrote about learning to love herself . . .

"I learned to love myself properly - finding out what I enjoyed in life, and adding more of it to my daily routines. As my self- love was building up, I found it easier to forgive the other person. I find that the more time and effort I put into my own life and self, the less I seem to need from the outside world or my partner. If I neglect myself a bit or if I am overtired, I am more susceptible to resurfacing old unhealthy patterns, rather than my new healthy patterns. Communicating one hundred percent with my current partner also helps! Basically I have found that by looking after my own needs first, I feel more confident, more love, and more empowered. It is only then that I have maximum capability of loving others."

Having a feeling of hope is very important in the healing process.

Here are another person's words and thoughts that you'll find helpful, inspirational and give you a new feeling of hope . . .

"I think really focusing on yourself and finding things you liked, which is something I am not used to at all, helped me heal. I always have someone in my life or am helping others, so to turn around and help myself, I just fell apart.

"When he left me, I wanted to end my life and just give up. However, I turned to good friends and I asked for help. I asked for time and I started finding things I liked. I started making a list of the things that I found to be important to me and started doing them. Financial independence was one. I never really had that and just handled it on my own and now own my own truck (I'm a girly-girl).

"I have really gotten out there and dated and met different kinds of people, some who were so wrong for me and some who weren't so wrong. Although I still battle codependence, at times I feel I'm winning and hope that through more time I will find the strength to ultimately believe I can be loved by me. That is the key. I also find people who love themselves and ask them how they do it. I notice that they are more relaxed because they aren't waiting for others to make it all better or worse. So really, I think time, good resources, and patience are the key. I am still scared to love, but I'm getting closer."

Here's another woman's powerful story about how she was able to move on after her divorce and breakup experience . . .

"I've been divorced for almost five years now. I was terribly hurt - and the main thing was time . . . but so much more! Only recently did I realize I was over him- finally. The last few years, I have tried to stay positive and busy. Self-talk helped (although hard to do at first)—'I like myself,' 'I love my body,' 'I am the best,' 'I deserve to not just breathe, but truly live!'

"I worked hard. Set goals. Worked out, and did a lot of reading. I spent time with friends, my children, but more importantly, I spent time with me . . . learning to love me, forgive me, and accept myself for who I am, who I want to become and how I want to get where I want to go.

"I started dating again two years ago and now have a special friend. Some of the courage has come from knowing who I am and being happy in my heart. Sometimes I feel so full of love. I'll just spill over but not really for anyone in particular . . . just because it feels good. I take the time to ask him questions and answering his along with my own. Hard to do sometimes, but I prefer to take a chance on being hurt rather than having so much fear that I would end up hurting myself and depriving potential love."

Finally, another person's story about what it meant to love herself . . .

If she can do it, so can you.

"After a very traumatic divorce, I dug deep down inside myself and decided to move to Florida where I had lived as a child, near my ocean. It took a lot of guts and determination. I had to make several sacrifices. I had my own business and I gave that up.

"I made a passionate commitment to not look backwards, because I was not going that way. I became mentally tough, not hard but tough! I began to know myself again. I read, I walked on my beach, I collected shells and I started a garden of them. Every shell was a prayer. I prayed a lot. I nurtured myself, I nurtured my dog, and I nurtured plants. I stopped nurturing other people for awhile. I took a break . . . I retreated in order that I might live again.

"I went to a few therapy sessions, and then I started to rebuild myself, and do things a little bit differently. I learned to say no. I stopped doing things that I was uncomfortable doing. I worked out a lot. I went from one thing to another, until finally I was so comfortable with me and what actually worked best, that I felt convicted that I could reenter the dating force without becoming a chameleon who sucked up my feelings to make others happy.

"Then I did something that was really out on a limb. I met someone over the internet. That took enormous courage, but I joined a reputable match service, one that had a small fee. I was very soon after blessed to meet my husband. We dated for a few months and his children became such a part of my life and he became a part of my children's lives.

"We were engaged after eighteen months because neither one of us was going anywhere else. We wanted to be together. We did not need each other, but we wanted each other. We were married 10 months later. He is not perfect but perfect for me. Sometimes he stretches me to be a better me, and sometimes he challenges me.

"I learned to be more realistic in my own expectations by knowing myself. I also learned that I can give and give enormously again, because I know how to love myself very well. It took courage to know myself and move forward. The love that came afterwards was the completion of my healing."

Chapter 48

How Long do You Wait before a new Relationship?

"How long should you wait before getting into another relationship?"

We're all always in relationships, but it just depends on what type of relationship you are open to having. In our opinion, there is not set amount of time for everyone.

The most important thing you should NOT do after a relationship breakup or divorce is to numb yourself from feeling and get into another relationship, repeating the same patterns over again, without starting your healing process.

Some people rush into another relationship just to fill the void and deny the pain that they are in. If this is something you are doing, we urge you NOT to do it.

Some people wait months or years to get into another serious relationship but that's not what Otto did. Otto got into a relationship almost immediately with another woman after the breakup of his first marriage. Even though he got into a relationship right away with another woman and not long after that the two of us found each other, it doesn't work out for the best for everyone who tries this.

What Otto did that was different from most people who get into another relationship right away is that he was willing to explore ALL of his emotions about his previous relationship and marriage to his ex-wife, even while being in these new relationships. We believe that while everything worked out fine for us with Otto getting into a new relationship right away, this is not our recommendation for most people.

If you take our advice and spend some time in reflection before getting into another relationship, here's something important to understand. We're not suggesting that you spend this time in reflection and rehash the whole thing over and over so that you can come up with ways to get back together. It's usually much too late for that after a breakup happens.

We're suggesting that you spend some time in reflection so you can look at what happened to your relationship that ended from a place of objective reality. You do this so that you can move forward in any future relationships from a new place of understanding for how you can do it differently the next time.

It's also important to take the time you need to grieve, if you need to, and to discover what you needed to learn from the relationship that just ended. Read and study about how to have great relationships and formulate your own vision for the type of relationship that you want to be in. If you don't do all of this, you will probably go into another relationship that might look different from the last one but has the same lessons attached to it that you haven't learned yet. We suggest that you lessen the pain in your life, especially the pain that usually comes with ending a relationship, by choosing to do the work needed to put yourself in a different frame of mind and different space before getting into another relationship.

Here's how we met . . .

We knew each other because we were in the same spiritual study group in our town, but we weren't attracted to each other during the

143

first couple of years that we were acquainted. As strange as it sounds, after we had both left our relationships, we suddenly felt a soul mate connection with each other. We felt like we were home with each other. Our attraction was immediate when the time was right, so waiting a certain amount of time was something we weren't willing to do. It wasn't an option for us. We felt like we had to be together and we've rarely left one another since the first night we realized our soul mate connection.

We both had a strong vision for what we wanted in a relationship, so we started ours in a very conscious way. We had begun our healing process and continued to do it together very deliberately.

For other people, it's different. For some people, getting into a new relationship right away after a breakup or divorce actually closes them down instead of providing a feeling of hope and possibilities. Be open to learning what's right for you and that comes from listening to what's inside you.

Here's how a new relationship helped this person heal . . .

> "Five months ago, I was an emotional wreck and had been suffering for three years in a loveless relationship. And then I met someone with whom I was able to make a distinction of what I wanted and what I didn't want in a relationship anymore. I opened my heart to genuine love and caring and started accepting that I had a deep desire for a meaningful and love-filled relationship.
>
> "I gave up my fantasy and illusions about the other guy, and faced the facts. I had to move on to something better, or stay stuck in pain for the rest of my life, and possibly ruin my life forever. I had to accept that my judgments were deluding me, and that I had to stand for what truly mattered to me, respect, genuine care, compassion and being reciprocated in a relationship.
>
> "I am still going through my healing process, but it's much better when I have someone who loves and supports me along the way."

Finally, here's one man's experience of needing to take time to heal before he got into another relationship . . .

"After having been married for a short time, my wife decided to have an affair. Of course, it was real trauma for me. It took me a little time to realize that in order to move on in my life, I had to find a way to make my head and heart come together. Counseling and a few talks with my preacher at the time gave me insight into why I hurt so much. It was not just the fact that she had cheated, but I also suffered the loss of trust.

"I took time away from women for a spell and learned to like myself before I entered into another relationship. When I did finally start dating again, I found someone who I could truly love. With her love and my learning, I came to realize that trust was the thing that I was hurting with the most. She understood and with many hours of talking and learning from one another, we are now in a relationship that is building still today."

Chapter 49
Why Do I Keep Failing at Relationships?

"Why do I keep FAILING in relationships and marriages if I keep following the conventional advice that everyone is giving me about 'getting back on the horse' right away?"

The reason this person, and maybe you too, keep failing is because you keep getting back on the horse and not doing anything differently to help you to stay on the horse longer, or for that matter, choose the right horse.

The question is not how soon or how long is appropriate to get into another relationship. The question is what are you going to do differently in your life right now and in your next relationship to create a different experience and one that is more in alignment with what you want?

If you have a reoccurring pattern of failing in relationships and marriages, you may not be clear within yourself about whether you truly want an intimate relationship or not at this time.

A deeper question you have to ask yourself is—"Do I really want to be in another intimate relationship or am I getting into a new relationship because this is what is expected?"

Examine your motivations. Is this what society, your friends and family say you should do or is this idea coming from a place within you? Do you have the belief that an intimate relationship will enrich your life or do you equate an intimate relationship with pain?

If you find that you are not ready for a new intimate relationship, even if others are telling you to get out there and date, we recommend that you take some time and do some inner work on yourself.

Here's what one man said about his experience . . .

> "I have jumped right into another relationship after a breakup only to discover that I was only using that new relationship as a distraction to forget about the pain I was in. So I think it's important to heal from the old relationship before beginning a new one. It also helps to have someone to talk to through the healing process, whether that is a good friend, family member or counselor. In my case, I see a counselor because I feel safer with an impartial person."

If you think you are ready to start dating, a second question to ask yourself is "What do I want from a relationship when I get it?" If you don't clearly know what you want, you may simply attract to you the same type of relationship that just ended. We suggest that you look deeply within yourself and identify the type of person you want to be with and the type of relationship you want to have. Ask yourself—"How do I want to be treated by my beloved?"

Here's what one woman discovered about her healing process and her path to the love she wanted . . .

"I went through a very painful breakup after living with and purchasing a home with my boyfriend. It took close to a year to heal enough to just start dating again. It took time and a decision (very important word, decision) that I was going to get what I wanted out of life and relationships. Time was key, but I made clear decisions – as difficult as they were – to focus on me. Walking, taking a sign language class, traveling, anything to get me out experiencing life again. Then I took some time to reflect, once the wound had healed enough, to see the good in my past relationship and note my mistakes. It took a long time to trust my instincts again, but eventually after trusting myself again, I met someone. We are now married and share a wonderful, connected love."

So, before you start dating again, decide if you really want a relationship, decide what kind of relationship you want, learn about how to have great relationships and take whatever time it takes for you to recognize and heal your destructive patterns and come into a feeling of possibility for what you want.

We suggest that you choose consciously what you want for your next experience and what you want your future to look like.

Chapter 50

How Do I Find a Loving Partner Again?

"How will you be able to find a loving partner again?"

Often, after a relationship ends, it looks hopeless to finding a loving partner that you want to be with. One of the keys is to not give up hope if you've decided that's what you want. People often don't attract partners they want to be with because they haven't healed from their past relationships, and deep inside, they do not believe that it's possible for them to have what they want.

Here's a woman's story of how she found a loving partner again . . .

"I had to heal from the loss of a twenty-three year marriage. It ended in divorce. Not my choice. I had worked very, very hard to save our relationship, but it was pretty much a one-way street.

"Since I had no choice but to carry on with my life in another direction, these are a few of the adjustments I made. I had to consider the well-being of my youngest child who was fourteen at the time. Making choices based on love for her (as well as myself) made it a little easier. I had been a stay at home mother, so I now had to completely change my way of supporting myself. I threw myself into my own business. It wasn't just any business, but one that focused all the love, energy and compassion I could muster. In other words, I had to find new meaning.

"There were of course all the negative emotional and financial repercussions of separation and divorce, but it was absolutely necessary to focus on the present and future rather than the past. My business venture and my daughter took all of my energy, and there was no new relationship for twelve years.

"Although I did not become very financially prosperous, I learned a tremendous amount about myself and life. I developed a much deeper spirituality in the process.

"Eventually, I met someone and we had a brief and turbulent affair, but it broke me free of the belief that I could never love again. As painful as this was, I learned what I did not want in a relationship anymore.

"Not long afterwards (within the year) I had the opportunity to become part of a very different type of person's life. I deliberately turned my inclinations in the opposite direction to where they were programmed to go. This relationship endures to this day, some ten years later. That isn't to say we don't have our ups and downs like everyone else, but it is a wiser more self-knowledgeable kind of union.

"Through these years and lessons, there is still more to learn I'm sure. One particularly important area that I am currently working on is the area of self-esteem and self-reliance. Codependency has taken a serious toll from the beginning, and it too needs to be turned around. This is unfinished business, but I know the direction that I must follow.

"We had to become whole ourselves before we could truly be with another. Perhaps others may accomplish this much more quickly than I have. Perhaps it's not about speed. The evolution of a soul takes its own time and all we can do is be open to the learning.

"Thus said, patience and forgiveness with ourselves and others, I believe, is of the utmost importance. Finally, I think, that you cannot hang your hat, your happiness or self-fulfillment on anyone else. They may be a beautiful, cherished and growth-inspiring part of your life, but ultimately you and your spiritual underpinnings walk together alone."

What a great story about how one woman took a chance, learned from it and took another, wiser chance at love and keeps on learning and growing!

How will you be able to find a loving partner again?

You do it by listening to what's inside you and taking it a step at a time. You do it by remaining open but doing what you need to do to heal yourself from your past hurts. You do it by learning to love yourself.

Chapter 51

Keeping Past Hurts in the Past

"How do you keep past hurts in the past and keep them from ruining new relationships?"

We believe that there's no such thing as failure in relationships, only lessons that you haven't learned yet. When thinking about the things that caused a marriage or relationship to break up, the best place to come from is from a place of curiosity, a place of wonder of what you can learn from this situation.

Instead of looking at a relationship that didn't work out as a failure, we would have you appreciate the relationship for what it did bring to your life. Maybe it taught you what you didn't want, maybe it taught you what you wanted more of—whatever the case, stop and take notice of what it taught you. No relationship was wasted time.

This isn't wishful thinking or us simply wanting to make you feel good. This is a powerful strategy for moving on from a breakup that can change your life. It changed our lives when we applied this new way of thinking to our situations and we know it can make a difference in yours.

When both of us realized what we learned from our previous marriages, we could come to a feeling of being grateful for having those experiences. When you realize the higher purpose of why you were together, you learn from the experience and you won't be as likely to carry the mistakes you made into a new relationship.

Know that we are always carrying our past into new relationships and situations. What we can learn to do is to consciously recognize when we are doing whatever it is we do that destroys our relationships and stop ourselves in our tracks. We can learn to recognize the signs of when we are going into our patterns and learn to flip the switch into acting from love and a more empowered place rather than fears from the past.

Here's what one person says about learning about her patterns . . .

"To me, the key to healing my past relationship was forgiving myself. After the denial, and anger with my partner, I realized that the real anger was coming from feelings about myself. Without learning how to forgive myself, and being open to learning more about the patterns I kept repeating in my relationships, I wasn't able to move on. I am still looking for a healthy relationship, but am no longer attached to that being the most important part of my life. It's just one of the many goals I want to accomplish."

We've talked about the stories we tell ourselves in previous sections of this book. Part of identifying your patterns is recognizing those stories that you constantly tell yourself that may be sabotaging your healing, your relationships and moving on with your life. You might be telling yourself that you will only be hurt again like your last partner hurt you or maybe it's a thought process that sends you into destructive patterns. Whatever it is, you have to identify them and heal it.

Early in our relationship, Susie found that she became jealous of Otto when they were in groups of people, especially women on a similar spiritual path as him. The story she told herself was that he would find someone more attractive and spiritual than she was. Because her ex-husband left her for another woman, she unconsciously carried the attitude that Otto too would leave her for someone else.

As you can imagine, the pattern resulting from this story certainly had the potential to damage our relationship. Susie became aware of this pattern and started becoming aware of when she began to feel fearful and out of control.

When she got those feelings, she breathed into that area of her body where she felt them and just allowed them to be there. She acknowledged that she felt afraid that the past would repeat itself but reminded herself that that was then and this was now. Since Otto was doing nothing to warrant the jealousy, she knew her work was to change what she told herself in these situations and to change the stories that she imagined.

Whether it's a belief that you will only be hurt again or it's a pattern that you know was detrimental in your last relationship—there's no easy way to stop doing it except one moment at a time. You have to be persistent and you have to allow yourself the time to heal, while making a little progress each time those old patterns come up.

Here's what one person says about healing the past . . .

"My boyfriend was very emotionally damaged after the relationship with his ex ended. They spent several years together and have two children. I knew he was very gun-shy when I met him and it took years of showing him love, even when he was difficult and resisted getting close to someone again, to make progress in our relationship. I think time, being shown consistent love and being given specific suggestions that helped unite everyone more (like us spending time regularly with his children) allowed him to finally start to love and trust again. We still have work to do, but many barriers have been transcended and many steps forward have been made."

You can have every intention in the world to not let the wounds from old relationships interfere with a new relationship, but they will creep in from time to time until they are healed. Accept that this is a work in progress and lovingly move on in your life, in whatever way is your next step.

Chapter 52

Staying in a Good Relationship with Your Kids

"How do you stay in a good relationship with children after the divorce? They might be attached to both parents and if one of the parents initiates the divorce, they might treat this step as a betrayal of their trust and love towards the initiator."

Here's what Otto says about this . . .

When I made the decision to leave my ex-wife, my son's mother, of course it was difficult for everyone. If I've learned anything about staying in a good relationship with children after the breakup or divorce, it's that you have to set your intentions for what you want and follow-through with those intentions. If having a great relationship with your children is what you want, then make that commitment to them and to yourself. Then live from that place where that commitment is.

"In my own life, in order to follow through on that intention to remain close to my son, I've made many decisions that I may not have made otherwise in order to keep my close relationship with him. Although I do not live with my son and his mother any longer, I spend as much time with him as many parents do who live with their children.

"My intention was to follow-through on what I told my son I would do and I have. I have attended his ball games, even though it might not be my visitation times with him. I have picked him up when I said I was going to. I made sure he knew he could call me on the telephone when he wanted to and talk with me. Since we share a love of baseball, our special thing to do together is to go to games together.

"In the first years after my divorce, my son was having a very rough time adjusting to my not living with him and his mom. I spent much of my time with him, showing him that I still loved him no matter what.

"When Susie and I came together, I did not introduce her to my son for a year. I will be forever grateful that she gave my son and me the space to be together by ourselves and to enjoy each other's company without her feeling left out. She did not have the expectation or rush into the idea that the three of us would be or needed to be a family and she allowed me to parent my son in all ways.

"So often step-family relationships are strained simply because not enough alone time is encouraged between the parent and their children. I do think that one of the reasons that I have the close relationship with my son today is that he and I both gave it the time, attention, and energy it needed to grow and thrive.

"One final thing about maintaining a close relationship with your children after a divorce—as difficult as it may be and no matter what has happened between you and your former partner, you have to honor the relationship your child has with the other parent, no matter how much you dislike that other person. The only exception may be when the children are in danger of physical or emotional abuse and that requires you to step in."

Although this was our experience and there are no right and wrong ways, what we do know is that it is possible for both parents to have a good relationship with the kids after a divorce. It takes courage to speak your truth, following through on what you say you're going to do and a lot of love in your heart to make it work.

Here's one woman's experience in moving on with a new relationship while maintaining a great relationship with her kids . . .

"I was married for twelve years, and had two children. My ex-husband and I were great friends. But as the years passed, I began to grow 'out of love.' I still loved and cared for him dearly as a best friend, but I could no longer bear to be intimate with him. Yet I still stayed in the marriage, and never told him of my feelings. I continued on the charade of the happy wife for about four years, thinking that my loss of love may just be a passing phase. But it wasn't. And the intensity of not wanting to be touched increased.

"Finally one day, when things had several months earlier begun to get rough between us, I decided it was time to reveal what had been going on inside of me. He was naturally very devastated and strange as it may sound, so was I. I came from a broken home, have never had a dad in my life, so I had always promised myself that when I married I would make it forever. Unfortunately things didn't pan out that way. After he moved out of our home, I went through months of depression and extreme guilt. I became suicidal. Finally I sought help from a wonderful psychologist. She helped me to focus again. Although the guilt of breaking up our family was still inside me, I was now able to manage it.

"He and I have remained very close friends through the whole separation and divorce. That has helped all of us, kids included, to overcome the pain of a family breakup. My dream is to have a marriage like my grandparents had, over fifty years of marital bliss. And even till the day my grandfather died, the two of them were so close and inseparable . . . like teenagers in love. That is my dream to have that in my life.

"Since all this happened, I have met a man. Although I fell in love with him, and he with me, I put up barriers and pushed him away for so long, out of fear of failure. But he is an extraordinary man, patient beyond what words can explain. He has, with his kind and gentle and patient nature, enabled me to open myself to love again. And although we are taking things very slowly, I can visualize myself growing old with this man. With more of his help, I think in time we will be able to start a life together, living together. But for now my focus is my kids, and making their life as pleasurable and carefree as possible . . . with both their mother and father in it . . . even if we are no longer a couple."

We realize that many children are raised by only one parent and that single parenting is not easy.

Here's one woman's story about what she did as a single parent to create a great relationship with her children after her divorce . . .

"As a single parent, raising two children, ages four and one, after my divorce was not easy. I was devastated and built a wall up around myself, not letting anyone inside. Thank God for my younger brother who had a family of his own and took the time to help me and my children. He was like a dad to them. With his many talks and compassion, he brought me back to life.

"There were two children who needed and counted on me to take care of them. Through his love, I was able to hold my head up high and love myself. It was difficult but I know today, I'm a better person because of it.

"It has been twenty-eight years since my divorce, and I have the greatest relationship with my son and daughter. Through my kids, who are both married and have families, I learned the real meaning of love."

Chapter 53

Strained Co-Parenting Issues

"How do you move on when you have to deal with strained co-parenting issues?"

S trained co-parenting issues that are a barrier to moving on are, in our opinion, a sign that there is still a good deal of personal healing work to be done as a result of the breakup or divorce.

If there are strained co-parenting issues, the first thing we would tell you is that the most important thing you can do is to focus on your children and how you can love, care for, and maintain a great relationship with them, no matter what.

If you and your ex are still experiencing a strained relationship because of co-parenting issues, then you should know that this is simply the continuation of many of the same issues, challenges and struggles that caused you to separate or divorce in the first place. The issues are just playing themselves out in different and sometimes uglier ways.

In our opinion, we do think it's possible to move on (and even have a great relationship with someone new) when there are children involved from a previous relationship or marriage.

The key is to be clear about what you want your relationship with your children to be like, both now and in the future. We also think it's a good idea to set an intention for what you want your relationship with your ex to be like.

We're not saying that you have to or would want to be best of friends with your ex, but the fact is, they are the mother or father of your child or children. No matter what is going on between the two of you, we think it's helpful and healthy to cultivate a respect and appreciation for that fact and the role that they played in bringing these precious beings into the world.

If you are clear about what you want all of these relationships to be like, then the process of moving on will be much easier. You'll know the kinds of things you'll have to do and the kinds of beliefs and attitudes you'll have to adopt in order to make your intentions a reality. This will also give you a better idea of the inner work you're going to have to do personally in order to continue the healing process and moving on.

Remember that none of us are perfect and we're all doing the best that we can do. Even if you've made what you thought were mistakes or have issues with your ex about a challenging co-parenting situation, this situation is probably happening because both of you want the best for your kids and you both have different ideas about what the best is for the children.

Our advice is to focus on the most important or common goal and that is creating a happy, healthy, loving and well-adjusted child who grows up to live in love, and not fear, as a result of your breakup or divorce.

Here's what one woman sees that she and her ex did wrong when they tried to co-parent their child . . .

"I don't think I ever moved on until after our son got a little older. It took less contact with my ex. We had joint custody and we had constant contact. He was involved with another person almost

---

immediately, then remarried and suddenly there was a third parent in the mix. Not a pretty situation. She and my ex-husband made decisions about our son and she was an equal partner in those decisions. There was a lot of confrontation and resentment on my part.

"How do you deal with the ex and how do you raise a child together? We didn't do it very well. Looking back on the situation, there should have been a meeting of the minds about how are we going to co-parent from the start.

"I've come in my growth as an individual to the point to where I can see that I should have insisted that we talk about the issues that came between us, but at that point in my life, I wasn't where I am today. I have just learned so many things about how you deal with confrontation and disagreements.

"I wish we would have come together and talked about our interactions—how we solved problems, how we dealt with holidays, finances, child support, educational meetings with teachers, living far apart.

"I could have done it successfully with just my ex but his new wife was strong and I was shut out of a lot of decisions. If there's a third person involved, there needs to be clear boundaries involved and there weren't in my case. I always felt that she was the force that made the decisions and my ex never said that this was not right. All those things should have been discussed in a contract—how we were going to communicate and make decisions for the best of the child."

While every co-parenting situation after a divorce is not this conflicted, this woman's story does give some food for thought if you are in this situation. Our experience has been that if you have as many co-parenting issues clearly defined as possible, you will be more successful and your children will recover and even thrive after the divorce.

If you need mediation to help you with this, get it. This is very important to your children's future, as well as your own.

Chapter 54

Knowing When You've Found the
Answer to Lessons Learned

"When do you know you've let go, moved on and found the answer to the lesson to be learned from that relationship?"

There are several ways we can address this question, but the most important thing we can share with you is that within every past relationship, there are usually not just one, but many lessons and ah-has that can be learned and gleaned by looking at (but not staying stuck in) your past relationships.

Within every relationship, past and present, there are potentially dozens or hundreds of personal and life lessons that could be learned by looking at your life and relationship with a particular person.

Sometimes for whatever reason, a particular person can seem to have an emotional or energetic hold on you that you can't quite shake off and other times the lessons come quickly and easily, without much emotional charge.

In our judgment, you will know that you have let go and found the answer to the lesson from that situation and that relationship when there is no longer a physical or emotional charge within you when you think about that other person or about the situation that has kept you stuck in fear, anger or pain.

You know you've let go and moved on when you begin to feel life again.

Here's one person's process for letting go, moving on and learning lessons that need to be learned from a past relationship . . .

"First there was denial . . . a numbness that puts you in between knowing and not knowing, where you know, yet you don't. Then one day, you wake up and you wonder what the hell you are doing. Then you pack up all the things that ever reminded you of the person, of the things you did together, of the fun and fights and presents and hopes. Then you cry. You cry like someone you love just died, because they did. You cry for yourself, for everything that you wanted and didn't get.

"Then you go out and do something nice for yourself, usually something extreme like chopping off your hair. Then you dance and drink and try to forget, but you never really forget. Not until one day, you wake up and wonder what the hell you are doing.

"Then you pack up all the stuff that you hid in your cupboard, grind them through the incinerator and realize you are ready to move on. Your foolish heart still flutters when you see someone who looks like him.

"When you hear he's getting married, you say, 'Oh, that's good' and somehow telling yourself the next one is always better sometimes works.

"When you finally realize that if he can't love you now, he never will, you'll know that you are ready to not forget, but to FORGET and move on."

As far as finding the answer to the lesson to be learned from the past relationship—there may not be one answer, and you may or may not be able to put your finger on what the answer is anyway.

For many people, they know that they have found the answer to the lesson to be learned from that relationship when their life begins to work again or maybe work for the first time. They are able to start creating their lives the way they want to create them.

Your breakup might be the catalyst and opportunity for you to begin the healing in your life that you know that you need to do.

Listen to one woman's story of healing her life . . .

"Having been a sexual abuse survivor from childhood up through my marriage, my self-image was zero when my husband walked out on me and our two children for another married co-worker. All my soul walked out that door that day. All our plans and goals in life were for the both of us and our children. I felt like a shell of a person when he left. My very first thought was of course to kill myself, but thank God, the fact I had two children to raise brought me to my senses in quick order.

"At first, I fasted and prayed for him to return, but after a week, God told me he would not. Having such low self-esteem, I first took all the blame for the breakup on myself. So I decided I was the one who needed work. I started buying every self-help book I could get my hands on. I probably read over thirty books during those first few months. I slowly felt better about myself.

"I love flowers and had always told my husband and kids not to bring them to my grave, but give them to me while I was alive. My husband had betrayed me with a rose as he lied to me about his affair. So I bought myself a little grocery store bouquet each Friday and that made me feel good.

"I must say my faith in God gave me the strength to continue. That is where most of my comfort came from. But as I worked on myself, I made it a practice to celebrate every little victory I made. Nothing big, just some really good self-talk, a pat on my back, or a new book.

"I moved from my home town, went back to college, graduated with a degree in Social Work and got a very lucrative job in government. I was actually seen as a leader by many people! Imagine that!

"I chose to remain alone for the next fifteen years to finish raising my children. Then in April 1997, I met my soul mate online and married him in thirty-three days. We have been married almost eight years now and couldn't be happier in our marriage.

"My divorce was one of two of the most traumatic times of my life, but if I had not gone through it and had I not worked and healed those issues which resulted from it, I would not be the person I am today and could not give to my husband now half of what I am capable of giving to him now."

Although there may be apprehension and fear, when you're ready and you've done your inner work, there's an internal decision to move forward.

"I allowed myself to go through the stages of grief. I cried, got angry, talked and analyzed the situation to death, then moved on. I had very good friends and family around me to help me get over the painful breakup. I kept a journal which was very useful, especially to look back on. After the initial grief, I tried to keep very busy. When I met the next man, I was very apprehensive and frightened, but decided to give it a go!"

Finally some words of wisdom from a woman who knows that she has learned her lessons and is open to continuing learning them . . .

"After two divorces and forty-three years of growth, I came to realize that my happiness cannot be dependent on having a man in my life. After reading helpful articles like yours and other books, I realized that happiness comes within. I also believe that God has a plan for us and that in the long run, that plan is for the best.

"I wouldn't take back any of the painful experiences of my marriages or other relationships, because those experiences helped me grow and learn. I moved on from my marriage breakups vowing to become a better person/partner and focus on internal happiness.

"It's a wonderful feeling knowing that I have total control over my own happiness and that it's not dependant on others. With that focus, I know I will be a better partner in any future relationship. I try to live by the saying 'I cannot control the actions of others, but I can control my reaction to them.'"

Chapter 55

Spirituality and Faith in Healing a Broken Heart

"What is the role of spirituality and faith in the process of healing a broken heart and getting over a relationship breakup or divorce?"

For many people who've gone through a relationship breakup or divorce, their faith in God (or whatever Higher Power) and spirituality seems to have been very instrumental in their healing process and in some cases and situations, has even sped up the healing process.

Here are a few reasons why . . .

For some people who've gone through a breakup or divorce, it helps them in the midst of a turbulent time in their life to feel like they are tapping into and being supported by someone or something greater than themselves.

Sometimes, when we go through extremely challenging times and situations (like a breakup or divorce), we may feel like we are personally, physically and emotionally exhausted and we can't take another step in our lives without crashing. When this happens, it's our faith and spiritual connection that can help us to go on and face another day.

Another way that faith and spirituality helps us in times like these is that being connected to God or Spirit helps us to feel a sense of love, compassion and caring in our lives about ourselves and others, even when we feel like we have been rejected and in pain at a level so deep that we hadn't known existed.

This faith and spiritual connectedness lets us know that no matter what has happened to us up until now, love still exists, it's not dead and you can have it as long as you are willing to open your heart to another once again.

We believe that one of the biggest (if not the biggest) reasons that we're all here on this earth and living the lives we're living is to have experiences that will literally force us to experience personal and spiritual growth and strengthen our connection with our Creator.

We're not the only ones who've talked about or written about this idea. Gary Zukav talked about the idea that we are here on what he calls earth school in his book *The Heart of The Soul.*

The earth school that Zukav is talking about is our actual environment we live in, which includes our friends, family, and everyone else we come in contact with. This includes everything else our five senses can experience.

In short, everything in our lives and every experience we ever have or will have is a tool that is offered to help us experience more and greater personal and spiritual growth.

In her book, *If Life is a Game, These are the Rules,* Cherie Carter Scott offers her "10 Rules For Living" which are all excellent. In her lesson seven, she talks about life lessons and we think these ideas particularly relate to anyone who is going through or has gone through a relationship breakup or divorce. She says that in life and living—"A lesson will be repeated until learned."

We know that these life lessons are part of our spiritual growth and if we keep this foremost in our minds, we have the confidence to know that we are on our particular life's path and we're okay, no matter what happens.

Throughout this book, in many different ways, we are giving you new ways to look at your breakup or divorce and how to best heal your broken heart. One of the most powerful paradigm shifts we are offering is the idea that there are always big lessons to be learned from all of your relationships, especially your relationships that are changing form and no longer serving you. The choice about whether you learn these lessons is always up to you, but it's been our experience that if you don't get the lesson, it will be repeated. You can count on it.

There's no question about it—going through a difficult time like a breakup or divorce can be tough. What we have discovered, both in our own lives and in our work with our relationship coaching clients, is that going through difficult times can bring you closer to God and your spiritual center or the pain can cause you to curse God and move away from your spiritual center.

In this book, we certainly don't want to tell you what your religious or spiritual beliefs should be.

What we do want to tell you is that in our personal lives and in the lives of thousands of our coaching clients, when we and others have fostered and moved toward a deeper spiritual connection, we have seemed to be able to heal our hearts more quickly than people who didn't have or develop that deeper spiritual connection.

Here's a person who healed by a deeper spiritual connection, among other things . . .

"I think for me the healing process was a matter of looking inward at myself, asking myself some questions. What do I want in life? What lesson or life teaching did I learn from this relationship?

170

How can I improve myself so that I am a better communicator in the next relationship?

"Also I took time to read books geared towards healing and spirituality. I think focusing more on my needs and interests helped me a great deal as I have neglected these needs in the relationship. Also, by talking to my ex-partner about what had happened and being able to remain friends and not blame him for the relationship ending, but accepting responsibility for my own part in the relationship helped me to heal.

"I started meditating, exercising and reading a lot more books on Buddhism and books by Dr. Dwayne Dyer and Deepak Chopra. All this assisted me greatly in my healing process. I would like to add in the past, I have not handled the ending of relationships well at all and in effect did all the 'wrong' things, i.e blaming the other, beating myself up, drinking in excess and looking for another partner immediately without giving myself any time on my own. It was sort of a desperate need to have someone in my life, a neediness.

"I have learned over time that this is not conducive to healing and only adds more insult to injury. I believe tuning in to ones self and taking time to find out what is going on inside is the best medicine."

This woman found the help she needed to move on by looking to her spiritual connection . . .

"If it wasn't for my spiritual background, I would probably still be angry about my life circumstances. You need to heal your heart before you can even move on and you need to forgive your mate before you move on.

"I'm not even divorced yet. I've lived in a loveless marriage for twenty-four years now. Why? Because I truly wanted my husband to love me. I tried to change that and even changed my personality just to get his approval. After twenty-four years of marriage, he is now allowing me to divorce him due to my stress.

"He wouldn't have even allowed it if it weren't for medical reasons. I am growing bald spots and haven't even turned forty-five yet. My body had no way to disperse my stress, so it affected my health. When he finally saw what he was doing to me, then he finally agreed.

"Why I couldn't be loved by him is still a mystery. I only know that it could have been his upbringing as a child. He never learned to properly love. I tried to reach him for so long, but finally realized that God can only change him. He has to be willing to change.

"Meanwhile, I've forgiven him already now knowing that God has a wonderful mate waiting for me in my near future. I'm hoping it will be a soul mate relationship with unconditional love. I would wait a lifetime for that kind of love. So I would say, trust God that he will bring you the desires of your heart but you have to give up the control of trying to change things yourself and just allow God to open the doors to your future. Let fate or destiny take over and allow personal change to happen. God doesn't want us to suffer in a loveless marriage or abused marriage or any other negative kind. He wants us to be happy with ourselves and then we can love others."

And finally, a message about how a woman's relationship with Spirit helped her to heal . . .

"I prayed and prayed and PRAYED. And, I backed it up with tangible things such as: going to the gym more regularly, creating positive affirmations for myself regarding letting go and moving on, doing things that made me LAUGH (shakes loose those attachments, don't chya know!), used techniques to switch obsessive mind-wandering regarding my ex to positive health-affirming habits, wrote comforting or funny songs, stayed clear of repeating old patterns that would draw me back into an unhealthy situation, wrote in my journal, got a massage, did girly stuff like manicures to feel girly-good about myself, sent the Light FOR THE HIGHEST GOOD to my ex and myself, observed my dreams for information and signs of healing, helped other people (very important to get out of my own stuff), danced, ate better, steered clear of dating too soon after the breakup, listened to a Spiritual tape called Mending a Broken Heart by John-Roger that I found helpful, slept with a great cuddly stuffed animal, dog-eared pages of my journal that were healing, uplifting moments I could refer back to, and PRAYED!

"Additionally, I tithed, which is a fantastic way to stay connected to my foundational relationship with Spirit especially in a time of challenge, and I also used a process called Seeding to keep me directed in my consciousness toward God and the Highest Good. The best description for seeding is at www.seeding.org.

"Thank God you asked me this question because I am going through a breakup right now and you just caused me to go over the stuff that works!!!"

Chapter 56

Stories about Moving On

To conclude this section, here are a number of stories and life experiences that further illustrate how to move on with your life. As you read these stories, take note of what might work for you to help you to move on.

A few years ago I went through an extremely difficult breakup. Unfortunately I worked with my ex, making it even harder since I had to see her day in and day out. For the first three or four days I was so depressed and sad that I was unable to look anyone in the face. I would just walk around and do my job staring at the floor.

"I did get over it, though I thought I never would. One thing I found that really helped was exercising. It really got my blood pumping which gave me a sense of happiness and well-being. Being complacent only perpetuated my depression, sending me deeper into the 'eternal' pit of sadness. Exercise gave me instant satisfaction, boosting my energy level and emotional status.

"I am also a musician, so I really started pouring myself into my music, writing some really cathartic material. I think just writing things down helped me put things in perspective. Once I got things out of me and onto paper, I found that to be a big first step in my healing process. Someone told me once that as soon as you put words onto paper you give them power.

"Of course my family was a huge support system for me. I went immediately to my mother's house and broke down. She was my shining light when all that surrounded me was a world of darkness and despair. The important thing is to have some tiny morsel of hope, just know that you WILL make it through this. Life WILL go on, and you WILL be happy again."

Expect that your new life will unfold in a wonderful, new way. Here is how one woman allowed her new life to unfold after her breakup and divorce . . .

"One of the things that helped me move on was actually moving from the people and city where I lived with my husband. It has been so positive to be away from that environment. A clean break was helpful for me.

"If there's any advice for moving on after a breakup that I would give, it would be to seek out things that support you. If you hold on and don't let go, you will miss wonderful opportunities that are put in your path.

"If you hold on and don't let go when your relationship is obviously over, your head is down. Your head has got to be up and you've got to recognize the things that come into your life. You have to acknowledge them— the people as well as the opportunities.

"Sometimes they are so subtle. If you are in an emotional state and hanging on to guilt or what was, you might not recognize them.

Learn to go with those opportunities. They're put in your path for a reason. Don't be afraid and over-analyze.

"When you start going with the opportunities, you start to get confirmation and positive things begin to happen. You start to become emotionally healthy.

"When I first came to the new town after my divorce, I stayed in a bed & breakfast. As it happened, the owner of the bed & breakfast was working on a house for resale that was perfect for me. I even got to choose the fixtures in the house!

"That was evidence for me that if you keep your head up and go with it, you'll find your next step in how to move on with your life."

Here's how another person healed and moved on . . .

"I turned to others for help. I joined a divorce support group, saw my doctor, who prescribed an antidepressant and had me see a counselor. They all helped and I no longer need any of those supports. Also I began a spiritual journey, which included classes in Wicca. My dental hygienist invited me to Christmas eve services at her church and I've been going ever since.

"I have taken classes in yoga, meditation, NLP, self-hypnosis, EFT, and some metaphysical things too. I like to read inspirational things such as your newsletter. I took training and became a volunteer for local dyslexia tutoring program. It made me feel better to help someone else. I recently heard a sermon about being a wounded healer and felt like it was given just for me!

"Life can be fun—lots to learn about and new things to do. I don't know that I'm completely 'healed,' but I am well on my way.

Doing what I was able to do for myself and asking others for help has empowered me. I don't have a man in my life right now. Maybe I never will. Right now, I just want to work on becoming a better me. If I am meant to have a soul mate, then the right person will appear when he is supposed to."

This woman found that forgiveness was key for her moving on in her life . . .

"After my live-in partner decided to have an on-going affair (even after I was fully aware of it), it took me nearly three months to move out of our place and leave him. I was still very hurt and extremely angry and bitter. I had gone alone, on a cruise vacation that was supposed to be for the two of us. It was during that week in which I had some quiet time to pray to my higher power. I did not want to hurt anymore and I wanted to move on and become healthy and happy again.

"In an answer to my prayers, I began reading such books as *A Return To Love*, *The Four Agreements* and other such spiritually enlightening books. I'm not normally a reader! I quickly learned how to forgive others, as well as myself. It may sound hokey but it's true.

"I remember the first time my ex had tracked me down to talk about the trouble he was having in the relationship he left me for. I felt sorry for him, but I listened to him and even gave him a bit of advice. It actually felt very fulfilling because I knew then that I had forgiven him and he no longer had any power over me. He was also going through his own personal hell and I felt bad for him, but I was no longer angry in anyway.

"I'll never forget what has happened and of course there were many more gory details, but my answer is to pray for the power of forgiveness and then offer it (forgiveness) to the person who has hurt and betrayed you, as well as to yourself. And do not try to stop yourself from giving love to them or anyone else. You may no longer be in love but remember that what we put out into the Universe, we receive ten-fold. And if we continue to cast out love and forgiveness, we overcome the pain and darkness. As we move on with our lives, we are freed from our pains and turmoil caused by that relationship."

Here's what another person did to move on . . .

"First I contacted all my old friends, even ones I had abandoned during the marriage, and asked for help. I told them that I really needed a friend during this, and thus started a support system. I avoided all contact with my ex, and kept that subject off limits with all my family and friends.

"I prepared a list of things I have control of—like diet, exercise, hobbies, etc—and created a list of things to do that were for my benefit so I would have something positive to focus on when I felt lonely and unsure of things. I read self-help books, and even started with a therapist, although friends are just as good.

"I avoided anyone or thing that made me feel less than good about myself or my situation. I tried new and even old activities, to see what the new single me might like - ballroom dancing, yoga classes, etc. I used a journal to write down all the fears and anxiety that plagued me, and used my support system to get the negative thoughts out, and gradually replaced them with Can Do statements.

"It took a long time to work on me, but after years of being everything to someone else, I was the most important thing I lost in the marriage, so I deserved to do something just for me. Once I created the person I wanted to be and was happy being, I then felt I could explore finding someone to share my happiness.

"That has not been easy either, but I had firm boundaries and a definite list of requirements, so I didn't waste much time with the wrong person, and didn't feel guilty about it.

"I am now in a loving, fulfilling relationship, with someone who is compatible in all my required areas, and we share the same core beliefs. You can't find the right person, until you know what you're looking for, and you can't know that until you know yourself really well. So consider your time after a divorce as a journey of self development and improvement, then you will be ready to move on and find the love you deserve, without settling for anything less."

Here's another moving on process . . .

"A breakup is very much like a death. It is the death of the idea of the two of you together. The picture or image of the life you had hoped for is gone. It can be devastating. Making sure you have a closure of sorts is THE most important thing, I think. Be able to at least know why things came apart, so you are not apt to repeat the same mistakes.

"Without understanding why or what caused the breakup, closure is next to impossible. How can you move on when you are in a constant struggle to understand what happened? Without closure, it can be like if you had a loved one that was missing without a body to bury. There is always that NOT KNOWING and it can make you crazy.

"Once you have closure, then at least you can go through the motions of life until you actually FEEL better and can actively join in once again. And who knows, while you are only going through the motions, someone might just like your sense of ease and ask you out. Once someone else is paying attention to you, it's MUCH easier to forget (at least for the moment) how your heart is broken. And every day will get easier. In the end, things always work out and as my mother says, 'If they aren't worked out, it's not the end.'"

Here's one woman's story of the breakup of her marriage and finding new love . . .

"I am going through a divorce that will be final soon, my initiative, and am currently involved with someone who I love very much. My situation may be a little different in that I fell out of love with my husband and have felt that way for many years. Though I tried to make it work for our daughter's sake, I just couldn't take the unhappiness anymore. So when my husband finally agreed to the divorce I was very much in need of feeling love from someone else on my level. My husband was very much like a big kid and would rather play than do any work or deal with any adult situations.

"I was not looking for someone when I met this guy at the gym. I did notice him the first day I started working out though and I had a feeling from the first moment I saw him that there was something about this guy. In fact, we didn't talk to each other for about two to three months until he finally came up to me and introduced himself. We went to dinner and we have been together ever since.

"I believe my mourning for a real relationship was going on during my marriage. I believe it takes time to realize the marriage has ended. You have to go through all those hard difficult times and all the emotions until you can move on. I am in counseling because I do have a lot of guilt with the situation as far as my daughter is concerned. I also know that I am on the mend and excited to start my new life."

Here's how one woman learned to love herself . . .

"I had a big crush on a guy at work but he was only interested in sex. I brought a shot glass for him from my Cancun trip and he only looked down on me, like he was doing me a favor or something. I was very depressed and wasn't feeling good about myself.

"My supervisor suggested that I see a counselor. I went and discovered I had a low self-esteem problem. The counselor gave me some advice on how to build my self- esteem by starting to go places on my own. I realized I was only in these bad relationships to keep from being lonely. I thought I needed a man to feel good about myself.

"I started to get involved in hobbies (swimming, sewing and bowling). I realized I had many good qualities inside and I learned to love myself. I discovered I didn't need a man to feel good about myself. I learned to stop focusing my attention on someone else but rather on myself. I accepted myself with faults and all.

"When I meet someone and that relationship breaks up, I learned to accept it and move on because it is not the end of the world. I realized the right person will come in time. The key is not to settle for someone to keep from being alone."

Listen to some wise words from someone who knows how to move forward in her life . . .

"At the end of any relationship that you have cherished, I believe it is only human nature to take the negative approaches to the breakup. 'What did I do wrong?' 'Why has this happened to me?' 'I'm a failure.' 'I'm never going to find anyone who can make me feel this way again etc, etc.

"I believe everyone experiences different degrees of emotions at the time of the breakup and have their own individual ways to get over it. The one cliché that still grates me is 'Time heals all wounds.' Crap!!! No matter how hard we try, we always will have the emotional scars from 'failed' relationships. Time just helps us cope with these challenging moments we encounter. And anyway, these moments help us to grow and form part of who we are (not that we see it that way at the time).

"So how do we move on? First, I asked for help from family and friends. I have suffered severe bouts of depression and knowing that at those times when you are close to doing harm to yourself, the help to get past that moment from your close friends and family is literally life-saving. Just by knowing that although the ex no longer wants you in their life, there are others out there who do and that idea helps to give a feeling of worth.

"I know of others who would get over the relationship by what I believe to be destructive behaviors like jumping into another relationship, sleeping around, alcohol, drugs etc. I have somehow figured out that to heal from a relationship breakup requires an internal audit and cleaning out rather than trying to ignore what has happened and what we are feeling.

"I have a couple of special spots I go to when I need to get back in touch with who I really am and what I want out of life. These spots all involve a quiet tranquil place in nature. One is by the ocean's edge and another is out in the bush.

"The hardest thing I have found to do is to flick the switch in your mind from dwelling on what has happened, to being more future orientated—where to go from here, how do I get to where to I want to be? There are often times when I have backslid, but I now know when this starts how to get back on track.

"At the end of the day, as much as our family and friends are a help at the start, the only sustainable change has to come from conscious decisions that we make for ourselves on the inside. As mentioned above, we also need to remember that we are human and there will be times we slide back into those moments of anger, fear, depression and self-doubt. This is on a sliding scale or a continuum and we need not punish ourselves when this happens."

Read how learning to play the drums helped this woman heal . . .

"I was able to heal my broken heart and learned to love again by tapping my overwhelming anxiety and hurt feelings into something meaningful. Let me explain. I was making, at that time my boyfriend of two years, a very special dinner. I had wine, filet, candles, etc. and just couldn't wait. Well, instead of him showing up for this special evening, he called to tell me it was over between us. It came completely unexpected. There was no solid explanation and nor would I get one. I was absolutely shattered. I had always been well-read on self-help books, which got me through many difficult breakups but this one, for some reason, was the icing on the cake.

"I became tremendously consumed with hurt and unanswered questions. I was unable to focus, sleep or do much of anything for days. My heart and spirit were broken but I knew that I needed to get it back. Life was too short to let this stop me from living a beautiful life. It was then, shortly after this, I decided to do something I always wanted to do but never did.

"I decided at age twenty-seven I would learn how to read music and play the drums. Sure, it may sound crazy, but within one year, I learned and the focus it required and the energy it allowed me to release by playing the drums was the best therapy I ever had! I would play every night and it made me sleep like a baby. Each day I would get better and my drum teacher always inspired me. He would give me things to practice, bands to see, clinics to attend, all of which slowly but surely gave me back my confidence that was so quickly taken away one horrible night.

"So, my suggestion to anyone going through a breakup is this . . .
No matter what age or no matter what others may think, do something you've always dreamed of but never thought possible. It's
absolutely liberating and is an amazing way to gain the confidence
to move on with life and love again."

Forgiveness helped another woman to move on . . .

"My ex-husband was verbally and physically abusive. He even
spent two nights in jail for abusing me. He took everything that
wasn't nailed down and moved to Florida. He told me I would
NEVER survive, he would ruin me so I would never have anything ever again and he would haunt me for the rest of my life.

"After I had already moved back to my own condo, the house was
foreclosed. He left me in debt of the tune of $300,000.00. I ended
up filing for bankruptcy and turning in my car to the bank. They
also foreclosed on my condo.

"I concentrated on the fact that he took, as I call it, all the stuff
and things but he didn't take my will to survive away. I went to
counseling to become stronger and re-establish myself. I left one
loan open at my credit union in order to rebuild my credit. I kept
focusing on my inner strength. And now after ten years, my credit
is repaired.

"For years, I carried such anger towards him until one day I
decided it was only hurting me. So I called him in Florida and
said, 'You can no longer hurt me and I forgive you for all you've
done to me. I no longer hate you.' He was speechless!!! I felt such
a burden lift from my heart and emotions by letting the past go
and moving on with my life in a more positive way. He was
shocked that I had the strength and courage to let it go. I told him
I'd pray for him too!

"I released myself to love again and have had two different long-term relationships that were sweet and wonderful. I now know it's best to forgive in your own heart and tell them you have forgiven them in order to move on for your own inner strength.

"One day I hope to marry again and have faith I'll find that special guy but right now my main focus is my son from my first marriage that is still in school another year. I've been dating a nice guy now for over three years and have learned many valuable lessons about love. Forgiveness is the first step and loving yourself enough to get away from an abusive person is the second."

More words of wisdom from someone who learned . . .

"This is what I did to move on. I knew that I had to stop and re-evaluate my life. We all need time to heal, instead of just going on the re-bound and hurting someone else, though we all have to go through the painful time of healing to start trusting again. I learned about me and ways to grow. I read, went to school, anything to better myself. But, I decided that I wasn't going to dwell on it and punish myself.

"But what really worked for me is that I decided that life goes on and I was going to live mine. I really made an effort to quit thinking about him and I found that once I did that, it really worked. I refused to let bitterness or not forgiving destroy me from the inside out; that can eat you up like a cancer.

"Yes, we have to go through a grieving process, but we can't stay there. We always need to move forward!! Just let it go and move on with your life. Life is so short and if we decide that we're going to enjoy the time we have left, isn't that better?!!

"I like the line in the song 'What a wonderful world we live in' –'Never let anyone rob you of your tomorrows.' Another quote I like from the song is 'Never let yesterday use up today!' (But to be honest, I learned this and so much more with age.) That's wisdom!!"

Some practical advice from someone who is healing from a breakup . . .

"I am currently in the process of trying to get over my ex. It's proving to be a very painful experience, and although I'm not sure it's foolproof, because like I said, I'm in the process, but there are a few things that have been helping out . . . A LOT!

"I make sure not to romanticize the past because I think that's the whole reason I tried to hold on for so long. I'm not even going to try the whole let's be friends thing because I know I won't be able to handle it. I will either end up right back in my going nowhere relationship or I'll end up rehashing all the pain I've worked so hard to cope with and move past.

"I try to surround myself with honest people who don't engage in manipulation and mind games. I know I'll move on at some point so why not do everything I can to start moving on right now. I don't want to end up bitter and I want to love again."

Read one man's advice on healing and moving on after a breakup . . .

"When I first got divorced in 1977, I was left on my own. My wife took the children and lived over a hundred miles from where I was which was what caused most of the heart ache because I couldn't see my children as often as I would have liked. I did see them every month or so and took them to my parents during my holidays, so I kept in touch as often as I could.

"As for my wife—well you know what they say, time heals. I started going out to ballroom dancing classes and met a lot of lovely people and gradually over time my pain went away. It wasn't for another ten years that I met the woman who became my second wife but sadly that came to an end fourteen years later. This time her two daughters who were in their late teens and early twenties stayed with me and supported me after she left which was a great help and comfort for me.

"At the time of her leaving, we were both enjoying line dancing a few times a week. I carried on line dancing and have made a lot of lovely friends, mostly females, which as you can imagine have helped me a lot.

"The most hurtful part about this separation compared to the first was that my second wife was still around and I kept seeing her with her new boyfriend which upset me quite a lot. As I said earlier, time heals and with the help of the two daughters and my friends from line dancing, I eventually got to a point where seeing my wife with or without her boyfriend didn't bother me any more.

"I'm still by myself four years later and still looking for that special someone. Any advice I would give to people in these situations would be to accept what's happened. Realize that it will take time to get over it and find a hobby or interest to take your mind off it and the most important thing is to go out and meet other people.

"Although, as I said, I haven't met my special lady yet, I feel privileged and lucky to have the friends that I do have which is helping me to get on and enjoy life."

And some final words of advice . . .

"The most important thing for me was to be accountable for my bad choices and to forgive my ex. I started a journal of my feelings during the whole recovery process. I wrote him letters but I didn't send them. He wouldn't have listened any more. I just got my feelings out. I then made a list of my mistakes and his and determined that I would not repeat mine and I would leave his in the past and let go of them. We still have to see each other because of the children and joint custody.

"I actually wrote a poem about a mental exercise that helped me heal. Here it is:

'Dawning'
'Taking my broken pencil from the place it lay on the floor where the desk you took away used to be, I wrote on the dusty, torn scrap of paper; my lost dreams and broken promises; One by one I documented them. With each press of the pencil, I broke more lead and sharpened it anew. With each new point made, I felt better as I released my shattered hopes and fears one last time. After I confessed these written words, I took the torn scraps and placed them into an individual balloon and filled it with helium. Marking the outside of the balloon with the written word it contained, I gathered the colorful balloons into a beautiful bouquet, took them out at dusk, releasing them forever into the sunset. I waited until they were no longer in sight. 'Farewell!' I shouted aloud until my shout became a song in the dawn of a brand new day.'

"The purpose for my writing is to bring others to a place of understanding the bumps in the road along the way. My author name is Thru_Her_Eyes and my work is at www.fanstory.com."

The process of healing your pain, finding the answer to the lesson of your past relationship, letting go, and moving on is not linear and may be like peeling an onion. It may not happen all at once. The process may be gradual. You may wake up one morning with a new optimism and enthusiasm for life that you didn't have before and then the next day you might be down again. You may find a new relationship and the lesson that you learned from your previous relationship may come up again so that you can deal with it one more time. You may also observe that finally one day you seem happier and lighter.

Keep your eyes open because books, courses and people will come into your path that will help you understand your lesson or lessons. You may know instantly what you were supposed to learn in your past relationship (and it might be many lessons) or you may discover it many years later and realize how you have grown.

Be easy with yourself and begin to find ways to enjoy your life. Remember, life is not a goal but a great, exciting adventure lived one moment at a time!

Resources to Help You Heal your Pain, Let Go and Move On

In this section of this book, we're going to explain several practical methods and give you some of the book and course titles that have helped us through the years to heal our pain, let go, and move on—not only from our relationship breakups but also at every step in our life journeys.

Try them out and then practice the ones that seem to work for you. Many libraries have the titles that we have listed so we encourage you to check them out also. We have compiled this section and give it to you with love and with the hope that, along with our words and the stories of others found in the previous sections, you will begin to see how magnificent life is once again, or maybe even for the first time. Our hope is that you will begin to live from the place of who you truly are, enjoying every minute of it!

1. "Sitting" – A simple way to begin meditating to release upsets, anxiety, difficult emotions and to find peace

One important way to help yourself heal is to begin a meditation practice. Meditation is something that can be completely separate from your religion or faith, although it certainly can be part of your spiritual practice if you want it to be. The practice of meditation on a regular basis can help calm you so that you are better able to let go and move forward from a more centered place and not from your habitual reactions.

Susie does this practice every day around 4:30 pm or 5:00 pm because that's when she needs to energize and sometimes to calm down so that she can totally enjoy and be present during the evening hours. If she had been feeling nervous or jangled before she sat down, all of that dissipates and she feels much calmer and clearer at the end of the meditation.

Whether it's this practice or another meditation practice, we suggest that you adopt some way that you can work into your day that will help you in truly magnificent and subtle ways. If you are new to meditation, this is a great way to start because it simply requires you to sit, breathe and just be for fifteen to twenty minutes each day. You can do it anywhere and it's a wonderful positive thing you can do for yourself!

Here's the practice:

Choose a quiet place where you won't be disturbed for fifteen to twenty minutes. Tell your family that you want some quiet time or put an out to lunch sign on your office door. Susie uses a small kitchen timer and sets it for whatever length of time she wants to meditate. That way, she won't have to think about the time while she's meditating.

Sit comfortably with your feet flat on the floor, your spine straight, and your hands in your lap. Begin breathing from your belly region, taking deep breaths. Your belly should extend out when you inhale, and move back toward your spine when you exhale. Just keep breathing in this way during the entire session, while focusing on your breath.

When thoughts come in (and they will), simply bring yourself back to focusing on your breath. Become the observer as your thoughts come and go, without being attached to them or trying to fix something. This is your time to rest, breathe and renew yourself.

If you get frustrated, know that this is normal and just keep breathing, allowing your frustration to be there. Usually, if you keep breathing, it will pass.

Please note that there are many, many ways to meditate. A walk in the woods or a run on the beach can be a meditation. We're suggesting that you adopt a practice that will help you to change the patterns in your life and move forward. Meditation certainly does that if you allow it.

If you want more information about creating a meditation practice, there are many great resources. For our favorites, go to http://www.howtohealyourbrokenheart.com/BrokenHeartResources.

2. "Power of Presence" exercise – Helping you deal with your emotions

At every step of your healing process, you need to be able to feel what you are feeling, acknowledge your feelings and either allow them to dissipate or take some conscious, appropriate action because of them.

The best way we know to learn to do this is to do a powerful exercise we've adapted from our friend and teacher, Dr. Belinda Gore, called the Power of Presence.

This is a powerful exercise because it helps you to get in contact with what's really going on inside of you. It gives you an opportunity to go within to find out what's underneath your pain, anger, abandonment or a thousand other feelings and to either act on those feelings or let them go.

Besides giving you a valuable way to deal with what you are feeling, this practice will help you to come into the present moment when your mind has made up stories about the fears of your future or has pulled you into your past.

What we're talking about is a way for you to see things as they really are—no better, no worse—and to help you to shift the feelings that come up to ones that are self-affirming and help you get through the next moment. We recommend that you practice this exercise whenever strong, uncomfortable thoughts and emotions come up for you and you want to shift into a more positive frame of mind.

Here's the exercise:

Find a comfortable place to sit, with your back straight and feet on the floor. Close your eyes. Take some breaths and bring that breath into your belly. Slow down and deepen your breathing. When you find thoughts coming into your mind (and they will), simply pull yourself back to focusing on your breathing.

1) The first step is to come into awareness about the chatter in your mind. Don't dwell on your thoughts. Just notice them, pause, breathe and let them go.

2) The second step is to observe what you are feeling about your situation and where you're feeling it in your body. Are you sad, mad, glad, alone, or afraid? Put one of those five emotions to what you're feeling. Notice where you are feeling this in your body. Is it in your belly area? In your head? In your back? Breathe into that area.

3) The third step is to allow whatever feeling is there to be there. Embrace the feeling and don't try to make it wrong, change it or work on it. Just breathe into that feeling and area of your body and just allow the feelings to be there.

4) The fourth step is acceptance. Bring an attitude of compassion and acceptance to whatever feeling that is coming up. This might not be an acceptable feeling for you but those feelings are there and by accepting them, you are acknowledging and contacting what's inside you.

5) The fifth step is to feel an active presence—to find guidance in your heart by quieting your mind so that you are able to speak and act from a centered place. This may not seem clear at first, but simply allow whatever is inside you to bubble up.

The guidance and information may come in the form of a strong feeling or perhaps like someone is speaking to you. There may not be anything that comes to you at first. Just be patient and allow whatever is to be there.

If you need to talk to someone and tell them what you are feeling, consider doing it. If it becomes clear that you need to take some action, take it from that clear, quiet place within you. If you don't need to do anything but be still, just be still.

Continue to do this until the strong, uncomfortable feelings have no more power over you in this moment. Repeat the exercise every time you get these feelings.

This is an exercise you can do to be with your feelings without trying to make them wrong, accepting and embracing them, without judging yourself. If you do it, you will feel better when those strong emotions start to overwhelm you!

3. Tonglen—Another way to get in touch with your feelings

Another powerful way we have found to get in touch with what you are feeling and allow the space for change and growth to take place is the practice of Tonglen. While it is similar to the Power of Presence exercise, Tonglen can take your transformation even deeper.

To explain how this works, we've included Susie's daughter Amy's description of how she uses this practice to help her be a better mother and bring more love into her heart. As you are reading her story, consider how you can use the practice to help transform your situation.

> "It was a Wednesday morning. I had prepared breakfast for my two young sons, cleared up dishes and was just shifting into my time, my daily yoga routine. Rather than go off to play by himself,

however, this day my youngest son, Micah, chose to stay in the room with me.

"He really wanted my attention and showed me this by talking, singing loudly, and hanging on my body as I tried to do yoga poses. As much as I tried to help him find another activity to do, he resisted. Granted, a four year old on my stomach added an extra stretch, but this was not the relaxing meditative space I very much needed for myself at that moment.

"Needless to say, I was frustrated and annoyed with Micah and resorted to putting one of his favorite videos into the VCR.

"Now my usual pattern in such a situation is to return to my yoga practice and push through the tension and annoyance; in other words, pretend the frustrating encounter didn't happen.

"But this day, I broke out of that pattern. For the past year or so, I've read several books by Buddhist teachers and have begun to practice a Buddhist technique called Tonglen. Recalling Pema Chodron's teachings of Tonglen, first I stopped doing yoga, laid on the floor and breathed.

"By focusing on my breath, I attempted to open my mind to nothingness, clearing my mind as much as I could. This can be especially difficult when we are feeling intense, as I was at that moment, but focusing on my breath really helped.

"Next, I began to get in touch with my annoyed, angry, and frustrated feelings as I inhaled. An important aspect of this part of the practice is that, in Chodron's words, you 'drop the story line' and focus on the underlying feelings.

"Without 'dropping the story line,' we can choose to go off on all kinds of tangents without really getting into the feelings. Again, I inhaled and as calmly as possible said to myself, 'I see that I am feeling angry and annoyed,' observing what was going on for me then.

"But this part of the practice is not just about getting rid of uncomfortable feelings. The goal is to 'touch' our feelings, to befriend those emotions.

"Cultivating love and compassion for myself was the next step I followed that day. After really feeling warm and expansive with love and compassion within myself, it was then time to extend those feelings to Micah.

"Tonglen is a Tibetan word meaning sending and taking. In the first parts of this practice, I took in the pain I was feeling and added breath or ventilation to that pain. But sending out my compassion to not only myself but to Micah, whom before had been a target of my annoyance, flowed smoothly at this point.

"I extended those feelings of compassion and love to Micah and acknowledged that just as I was working with discomforts of a headache that morning, he was not feeling well either and it came to me that he has only had four years to work on how to handle his feelings while I have had thirty-four years!

"I really felt my anger towards him dissolve. It wasn't denied. I was able to peacefully process and let go of those feelings.

"But Tonglen doesn't stop with yourself or the person you are irritated with, so I continued extending compassion and love. I added more and more people in my family, friends, people I don't know, and finally the entire Earth and all those who dwell upon it. I saw all of us glowing with love and compassion.

"It felt really good to do this. My aspiration is that I can continue to find the clarity to breathe through those very moments where I am about to raise my voice or get really angry towards my children or towards anyone.

"I continue to practice Tonglen more and more frequently, when I feel triggered by someone or a situation. As soon as I can identify that I am out of sorts, I begin to breathe and clear my mind in preparation to touch and be at ease with those uncomfortable feelings, before moving into cultivating love and compassion.

"This is never easy, but I have found it profoundly important in my life as a parent, partner, and human living on this planet."

To learn more about Tonglen, get Pema Chodron's book *Awakening Compassion: Meditation Practice For Difficult Times.*

There are a number of books and resources that we have found helpful in changing your thoughts and beliefs from limiting ones to ones that will empower you. Here are the resources that we recommend . . .

4. EFT-Emotional Freedom Technique

Emotional Freedom Technique, also known as EFT, is a process for making positive changes in your life. It combines verbal statements and holding or tapping energetic points on the body. This helps blocked or negative energy move and allows you to balance yourself on all levels.

EFT is actually fairly easy to learn, but more complex than we can go into in this section of the book. There are many great resources available for learning to use EFT quickly and easily. You'll find our favorites listed on our Resource page at: http://www.howtohealyour-brokenheart.com/BrokenHeartResources

5. How to change your self-talk and the stories you tell yourself

One of the best techniques that we've found to change your life is to change what you say to yourself. Whether you realize it or not, you are constantly talking to yourself about everything you encounter, about your past and about your future. If you can change what you say to yourself, you can truly begin to open to the possibilities of an empowered present and future, with more love in your life than you ever imagined possible.

One of the best books we recommend to help you with this is *What to Say When You Talk to Yourself* by Shad Helmstatter. It gives step-by-step instructions on how to change your self-talk. Use Helmstatter's method and you will see changes in your life.

Two other valuable books that have helped us to view what's going on in our lives more objectively, without making more or less of the present circumstances, are *I Need Your Love—Is that True?* and *Loving What Is: Four Questions that Can Change Your Life* by Byron Katie.

These books both have the power to help you identify the stories you run in your head about what's happening in your life, what happened in the past or what may happen in the future. They also help you to see the events in your life differently, allowing you to lovingly take responsibility for what's happened, without blaming yourself or anyone else. Katie teaches you how to love through your pain, if you are open to her teachings. We use her ideas in our coaching and in our personal lives and recommend these books to you.

Another book that asks penetrating questions to help you to stand in your truth about yourself is *The Right Questions* by Debbie Ford. Ford challenges us to wake up from our unconscious thought patterns and behaviors so we are able to discover more powerful ways of being.

If you want a great process to help you to get to the bottom of your conflicts with other people and your upsets, *You're Never Upset for the Reason You Think: The Cure for the Common Upset* by Paul and Layne Cutright is an excellent resource. In this book, they outline a very effective process for helping you get to the bottom of what is upsetting you and a way to work through the upset. We've used their process and we highly recommend it.

6. What do you do when you get stuck and want to sink back into your previous ways of thinking and being?

Many of the resources we've listed above can help you get unstuck, but the information that has had the most impact in this area is *Getting Unstuck: Breaking Your Habitual Patterns and Encountering Naked Reality* by Pema Chodron. This 3-part audio cd set is a straight-shooting, down-to-earth, presentation that helps you to understand first, why you get stuck in unhealthy thoughts, beliefs and actions, and then how to stop doing it. This is very powerful information that you can listen to again and again to keep you on track.

7. How to consciously create your life the way you want

Whether you realize it or not, you are creating your life the way it is in every single moment. In order to create the life you truly want, you have to learn how to create consciously and purposefully. Some people refer to the process of creating your life the way you want as manifesting.

The information about manifesting that we have used the most has been the teachings of Abraham, and *Ask and it is Given: Learning to Manifest Your Desires* by Esther and Jerry Hicks is a great book to get you started.

A couple of other wonderful resources on manifesting are *The Power of Intention: Learning to Co-create Your World Your Way* by Dr. Wayne Dyer and *The Attractor Factor* by Dr. Joe Vitale.

If you are interested and ready to attract a partner to you who is more in alignment with what you want in life, we've written a book called *The Relationship Attractor Factor* and a course called *The 7 Proven Secrets to Attracting Your Perfect Partner* that you may be interested in. You can find those on our website http://www.howtohealyourbrokenheart.com/BrokenHeartResources

8. How to become more emotionally aware

We have been greatly impacted by the works of Gary Zukav, especially *Seat of the Soul.* His book, *The Heart of the Soul: Emotional Awareness,* speaks to how to deal with intense emotions and emotional patterns when they come up. His book will help bring clarity to what you are feeling and give you healthy ways to use your emotions for your personal and spiritual growth.

9. How to make completions that have kept you from moving forward in your life and relationships

Most of us have an awareness of things that have been left unsaid that need to be said or things that need to be done that weren't done. We call these incompletions.

Incompletions can be a number of different things, such as unsaid words, broken promises, unkind acts, anger and resentment toward someone, or even not forgiving someone or yourself.

What we sometimes don't realize is that these incompletions keep us from what we want in our lives and our relationships because we're holding on to our negative thoughts which are usually anchored in the past. These negative thoughts usually keep us from imaging and intending what is truly possible, what we want in our lives and allowing us to let go and move on. They keep us stuck in the past.

Completions happen when we do or say something that allows us (or someone else) to feel complete about one or more situations where we may have been stuck.

If you make a completion about anyone or anything in your life, it can be very therapeutic, as well as a relief, for you and for the other person, as well, when you do.

Cathy took one of our courses and told us later that she had made two completions. By doing them, she has created space for something wonderful to happen and is moving forward to having what she wants in her life. She returned all of one man's things that were left at her house, including a computer, several months after they had broken their relationship. Also, she decided to break it off with a married man she'd been seeing every now and then for years. These things from a former lover and the relationship that wasn't going anywhere were holding her back from being with someone who could love her the way she wanted to be loved.

Completions aren't always as dramatic as Cathy's, but they always free up energy for something more wonderful and powerful to come into our lives.

Completions can take many forms. At the beginning of our relationship, the two of us did several completions to let our previous spouses go so that we could start fresh with our relationship. We did a completion ceremony that we called the ring toss at Bald Head Cliffs in Maine. As we stood on the edge of the cliffs above the water, we blessed and thanked our previous spouses and threw our wedding rings into the sea.

In another ceremony, Otto burned a number of audio cd's that he had listened to as he was deciding whether to leave his previous marriage or not. By burning these cd's, he released many of the negative feelings that had been trapped in his body that he held onto from that time in his life.

Completions can take many forms. A completion may involve speaking to the other person or it may not. If speaking to the other person is not possible or unsafe, a completion can take the form of a written letter if you need to say words that you've never said. You can then either mail it or burn it, depending on what will serve the highest good for both of you.

Although we encourage you to speak or write what is or has been true for you, we also encourage you to take your share of responsibility for what happened in the past. Even though you may not be ready to completely forgive the person, it is helpful for you to get to the place where you can realize how you have grown because of the situation. Remember, revenge is not a good reason to just blame and criticize the other person, saying or doing something that you may regret later and serves no healthy purpose.

Your incompletions keep you tied to the past. Our recommendation is to do something to cut those ties and allow those people to leave your life or change your relationship with that person to one that fits the life you envision for yourself.

Your completion may mean doing some forgiveness work, even though you may think that you have forgiven this person in the past. There are many books out there on forgiveness and one that is particularly effective is *Radical Forgiveness: Making Room for the Miracle* by Colin C. Tipping.

10. What does it mean to wake up to consciousness?

It's been our experience that most people are living their lives primarily on autopilot and if you start waking up to consciousness, your life will simply work better. Becoming more aware of your thoughts, feelings, emotions, intentions, goals, dreams and the things within you that are preventing you from creating what you want in your life are all part of waking up to consciousness.

There are many great resources that we can recommend for becoming more conscious, awake and aware in your life. Waking up is a journey and not a destination. With that in mind, below you'll find a couple of recommendations and many more at our resource page, http://www.howtohealyourbrokenheart.com/BrokenHeartResources

The Voice of Knowledge: A Practical Guide to Inner Peace by Don Miguel Ruiz guides us to knowing who we truly are on our path to inner peace. Any book by Ruiz is well-worth reading and his words are well-worth living by.

Kosmic Consciousness by Ken Wilbur dramatically changed the way we looked at ourselves and others around us. We highly recommend Wibur's teachings and this audio cd set.

What the Bleep Do We Know? is a very powerful film that explains some of the mysteries in life in a way that is understandable and based on scientific facts. We watch this film regularly to remind us of who we are and why we are here. We highly recommend this resource.

11.   Explanation about chakras

We've made a reference in this book about chakras and we promised you a simple explanation to explain what they are. There are several places in your physical body that correlate to specific ideas, issues, emotions and challenges that we call energy centers or chakras.

For example, whenever you feel fear or resistance about something or someone, very often you will feel a physical sensation of upset in your stomach or solar plexus area. You might even get sick to your stomach. These physical feelings in your stomach area may be the chakra in that area of your body doing its job, giving you information about what you are feeling and calling your attention to the issue.

For a more exact definition—Chakra is a Sanskrit word meaning wheel or disk and is one of the seven major centers of spiritual energy in the human body according to yoga philosophy. Each of these centers correlates to major nerve ganglia branching from the spinal column. They are specific locations within our energy system for the sensations, emotions, thoughts, memories and other nonphysical experiences. Chakras also correlate to colors, sounds, body functions, and much more.

There are a lot of books and websites filled with information about chakras. If you are interested in learning more about the human energy field and how chakras work, one good source is *Hands of Light: A Guide to Healing Through The Human Energy Field* by Barbara Ann Brennan.

We hope these resources, and the ones listed on our website, give you food for thought as you make your healing journey. It's been our pleasure to be with you and if we can help you further, let us know.

Many blessings for a happy, joyful life filled with love,

Susie and Otto

About Susie and Otto

Susie and Otto Collins are married relationship and life success coaches from South Central Ohio who spend their time sharing with others how to create more conscious, connected and loving relationships and lives.

Together, they are the authors of books, tapes and over two hundred published articles on relationships. Their book titles include *Should You Stay or Should You Go? Creating Relationship Magic, Communication Magic, Creating Relationship Trust, Relationship Attractor Factor, 7 Proven Secrets for Attracting Your Perfect Partner, How to Heal Your Broken Heart* and *No More Jealousy*.

For over thirty years, Susie has been a student of relationships, spirituality, energy and the life force. Her search for physical, emotional and spiritual healing has led her to the study of Polarity Therapy, cranio-sacral therapy, reflexology, Hatha Yoga, the Enneagram, and much more. Her formal training includes a Bachelor of Science degree in education, a Masters degree in Library Science, is a Registered Polarity Therapy Practitioner with the American Polarity Therapy Association and a Certified Comprehensive Coach. Susie is a veteran teacher and university librarian with over thirty years experience teaching in the public schools and university classes. On the university level, she's taught courses in Education, Communications and currently teaches a Women's Studies course.

Otto has spent over twenty years as a successful salesperson and marketer of a variety of products and services. Many years ago, as a result of pondering three of life's greatest questions— Who am I, Why am I here and What's this all about— Otto turned his life's focus to bear on the practice and study of spirituality, personal growth and relationships.

They passionately believe that life can be lived in a joyful, conscious, loving way and are committed to helping others to experience the potential of what is possible in their own lives and relationships. The desire to be loved the way they wanted to be loved took each of them on a journey of discovery of how to create the relationship of their dreams. They believe Spirit put them together for their own personal growth and to shine the light of hope for others. Their goal is to help others create outstanding lives and passionate, alive, connected relationships.

For well over twenty years, both Susie and Otto have immersed themselves in the study of personal and spiritual growth. Their primary focus has been the study of creating outstanding relationships of all kinds.

Susie and Otto's formal coaching and relationships training has been from The Hendricks Institute and Comprehensive Coaching U. For many years, Susie and Otto have been students of what makes relationships work and they continue to share what they have learned through their books, tapes, web sites, workshops, seminars and daily lives.

They write a free weekly online, content-rich newsletter that offers proven, practical tips and ideas for solving relationship problems and challenges that reaches almost forty thousand people in over forty-seven countries. They speak from their own experience and what they have learned from their relationship coaching practice clients, teaching people how to create relationships that last and ones that are filled with joy, passion, connection and love.

Contact Info

For more info about working with Susie or Otto personally to improve your relationships and have them be your Relationship or Life Coach, call them at 740-772-2279, email info@collinspartners.com or visit their website.

www.RelationshipGold.com

"FREE Relationship Mini-Course"

"Discover Susie and Otto Collins' Amazing Secrets For Creating a Closer, More Connected and Loving Relationship!"

Sign Up For Our FREE 5-Day Email Mini-Course:

This Course Will Teach You . . .

- What is the #1 way to improve communication in your relationships?
- What are the secrets to getting what you want in your life and your relationships?
- How can you master the most important relationship skill you need to develop?
- How can you build more trust in your relationships?
- How can you say what you want to your partner in a way that it can be heard?

Get this FREE Relationship Mini-Course by visiting . . .

http://www.FreeRelationshipCourse.com

No More Jealousy

A complete course including a 152 page book and 4 audios. This new course is for anyone who wants to overcome and eliminate jealousy from their relationships and their lives. For more information about this course, visit:
http://www.NoMoreJealousy.com

7 Proven Secrets for Attracting Your Perfect Partner

If you're ready, this course reveals our proven step-by-step formula for attracting your perfect partner and bringing more love into your life.
http://www.PerfectPartnerNow.com

Creating Relationship Trust

Of all the qualities that make up a good relationship, trust is undeniably the most important. It's the one quality that a relationship simply can't survive without. Discover the relationship secrets for building trust and dramatically improving your relationships. Visit http://www.relationshiptrust.com

Communication Magic

Discover the secrets to immediately improving communication in all your relationships and to create a lifetime of love. Visit
http://www.communication-magic.com

Relationship Attractor Factor

7 simple steps to attracting and keeping the love you want. For more information, visit http://www.RelationshipAttractorFactor.com

Should You Stay or Should You Go?

Susie and Otto's break-through process for helping anyone make the best decision possible about whether to stay in or leave a relationship.
For more information, visit: http://www.StayorGo.com.

Printed in the United States
205980BV00003B/9/A